# TOMORROW'S OFFICE TODAY:
## managing technological change

# TOMORROW'S OFFICE TODAY:

*managing*
*technological*
*change*

D.W. Birchall
and
V.J. Hammond

A HALSTED PRESS BOOK

## JOHN WILEY & SONS

*New York*

Published in the U.S.A.
by Halsted Press, a Division of
John Wiley & Sons, Inc., New York

*First published 1981*

Set in Baskerville

ISBN 0 470 27236 8

# Contents

# *Preface*

During the next decade the challenge facing those concerned with managing offices will be how to reap the benefits of new technology whilst maintaining a highly motivated, happy and effective staff. This book is not concerned with predictions about the numbers of office staff in 1990. It is concerned with helping managers, trainers, organisation and methods specialists and others as they take the inevitable small steps of progress. The book aims particularly to help the practising manager anticipate and plan to overcome the many issues raised by changing technology.

If there is one thing that is certain about the next decade it is that offices will become even more varied in scope and in the range of sophistication of systems. The manager of tomorrow's office will be a key figure in the information processing network, but the manager as well as the staff will need to be versatile. Not only will all involved have to be multiskilled, but they will almost certainly have to communicate with people using different levels of technology. Therefore the office will offer many challenges for those who organise, manage and work in it. Although there are many forecasts about the rapid rate of progress, there are counterbalancing factors. It is more likely that change will evolve, probably in a piecemeal manner, over several years. It will be more important for office managers to plan the direction as well as the detail of change. It will be necessary to have a buying policy that encourages the purchase of equipment which extends opportunities, rather than equipment which closes options. The change process may be a long one. Different parts of this book may therefore be relevant for different stages of the introduction of tomorrow's office. However the preparation for tomorrow lies in today.

Some books are meant to be read from cover to cover, others are intended for reference. Although this book can be read straight through, the short summaries at the end of each chapter are intended to help the busy manager decide whether the issues are of current priority. Similarly managers may find some cases more relevant to their situation than others. Trainers too will find some make good discussion documents for training concerned with the implementation of change. An effective way of using this book is therefore to skim through it to become familiar with its organisation and scope, noting relevant cases for particular attention, and then to read the appropriate chapters in more detail.

Many managers have given help and advice in the preparation of this book. Some of their experiences are included in the case studies. The cases all concern managers practising today, some who are coping with the demands of a technology thrust upon them and others who can anticipate benefits but who are anxious about how staff will adapt to the new skills. We believe their experience is meaningful and will be helpful to many other readers faced with similar situations.

# Acknowledgements

We wish to express our thanks to the Petroleum Industry Training Board and the Henley Work Research Group for support and encouragement in the preparation of this book and particularly with regard to a project undertaken in the oil industry. We are most grateful to the Board for approval to include this material.

We also thank the following companies for their co-operation, particularly with regard to examples of change situations:

Amoco UK Limited
Appleyard Fuel Service Limited
British Petroleum Company Limited
Century Oils Group Limited
Alexander Duckham and Company Limited
Elf Oil Exploration and Production UK Limited
Esso Petroleum Company Limited
Mobil Data Services Limited
Shell UK Limited
Shell UK Oil Limited

Particularly, our thanks are due to all those managers and their staff whose practical experience, successes and difficulties in introducing change will, we feel, be of interest to those who read this book.

Finally, we are most grateful to Miss Claire Collins for typing the manuscript.

D.W. BIRCHALL
V.J. HAMMOND

13.50

CHAPTER 1

# Technology in the office

In this book we examine change as it currently affects people employed in office work. We also look at how future changes, particularly those resulting from the adoption of new office technology, are likely to affect work and those engaged in it. We aim to give practical guidance to managers and staff who are either involved at present in implementing change or are interested in how they might influence and manage future office innovation.

We have drawn particularly upon the experience of practising managers involved in implementing changes and have considered the problems encountered in relation to the new systems themselves as well as the staff involved. Based on this practical experience we have produced guidelines to assist others facing similar challenges.

As a starting point, in this first chapter, we present an overview of new office technology and how it has developed. We review briefly the type of equipment available and the likely impact upon work of its adoption.

## The development of office equipment

Undoubtedly, readers will be familiar with most of the equipment available in the traditional office. Much of this equipment has been developed considerably during this century, e.g. mechanical devices such as typewriters and accounting machines have been replaced to some degree by electromechanical devices and later by electronic versions. The developments in technology and their widespread use have been gradual. Earlier technological developments were confined to discrete pieces of equipment with specific functions, e.g. typewriters and calculators. The increased application of electronic devices and the opportunities for mass-production assembly methods have contributed considerably to the rapidly falling cost of this equipment. This, in turn, has led to its widespread availability at work, particularly in the case of

1

electronic calculators. Whereas at early stages in the mechnisation of offices adding machines were confined to specialist departments, now most managers have a personal electronic calculator, and its use has been absorbed into the manager's everyday routine. The use of such equipment has undoubtedly improved the performance capability of individual managers without having had much effect on the way work is organised.

However, the same cannot be said generally about the use of computers in organisations. Computers represent automation in the office, compared with the adding machine or simple calculator which previously mechanised certain tasks. Computers have the capacity to be programmed to automatically carry out office routines. The introduction of computers into organisations created some new tasks, made others obsolete and resulted generally in substantial re-organisation of clerical work procedures.

The latest surge of innovation, the much publicised microelectronics phase, is likely to have a much more profound effect on office work than anything that has gone before. Undoubtedly, microprocessors could revolutionise offices, not only in the way tasks are performed but the whole concept of office work.

The new technology is attractive for many reasons. The new equipment, employing microprocessors, has the capacity in a relatively small space to store and manipulate large volumes of information. This can be achieved at a cost that is a fraction of that of comparable mainframe computer operations even as recently as those of ten years ago. As a direct result of the low cost it is economic to program tasks which until recently were considered uneconomic because of their complexity. Such tasks can be performed not only more economically by microprocessors when compared to humans, but also more accurately and quicker. The reduced space requirement of this new equipment compared with more traditional mainframe computers makes it possible to locate it in the office alongside the staff involved in its use. The low cost makes it feasible to provide managers and others with their own equipment interlinked with other systems.

It seems likely that the impact of microelectronics will be felt as strongly in offices as in any other function. In this time of change, not only the jobs of office staff are likely to change, but also those of managers and technical specialists. The changes will probably affect not only those engaged in large organisations, industry, commerce and public authorities, but also those employed in medium and small businesses. Where traditionally the clerk has carried out adding, typing, collating, mailing, sorting and filing tasks, machines are capable already of processing this work with little human intervention; thus the number of clerks engaged in such activities could be reduced drastically.

The speed and accuracy of processing makes machines attractive to

2

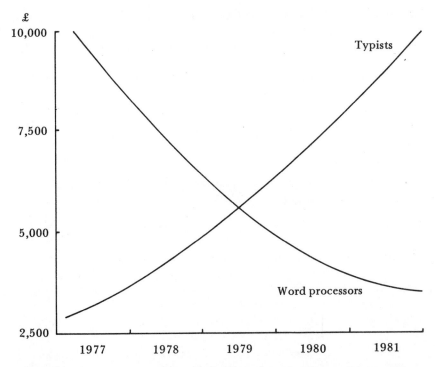

**EXHIBIT 1** An indication of the relative costs of employing traditional typists and word processors. *Source: Office Technology: a Trade Union Response,* Association of Professional, Executive, Clerical and Computer Staff, London (1979)

employers. The rapidly falling cost in real terms of equipment increases its desirability. Exhibit 1 illustrates the relative economics of employing equipment versus personnel for one office task, that of typing. Cost predictions of this type make it increasingly likely that microelectronic technology will become a viable, and indeed necessary, feature of office work.

Many of the new machines are versatile, they can be programmed to perform a wide range of tasks as well as linked with other equipment to permit the flow of information between systems. This opportunity offered by microelectronic equipment to combine completely different types of activities and also to sort and extract information previously too expensive to collect manually, is likely to have an even greater impact on the rate at which microtechnology is introduced than the economic considerations discussed earlier.

If, as it is often argued, knowledge is the basis of power for organisations, then the business with a highly responsive and accurate intelligence network will have advantages over competitors.

Considerations such as these will make many organisations of all sizes and forms look to advanced technology to provide, at a realistic cost, more accurate and detailed management information. They will use it to facilitate improved planning and control as well as to assist in directly controlling expenditure on office and administrative functions. In all forms of organisation increasing attention is likely to be paid to cost-effectiveness, and the office is not excluded from this requirement because of its role as a support function. It will be expected to make a contribution to the more effective running of the organisation and new technologies will be an important factor in meeting these demands.

## General effect on staff

As the use of technology in the office increases, so the jobs of clerks and other junior staff will change. They are likely to need new or different skills, authority and responsibility levels may need reconsideration and changes may be necessary in the supervisory structure. These and other issues will have to be resolved in the planning and implementation phase of introducing new technology. The problems experienced by the managers involved in the cases described later will not be atypical of those faced by many other managers and their staff when new equipment is being introduced. An awareness of the issues and problems can serve to alert managers embarking upon technological change. The approaches proposed later emphasise the need to take account of staff satisfaction and achievement at work. This is based on the assumption that technical efficiency only results in efficient operations where staff are also motivated to work efficiently.

In addition to changes in the jobs of office staff, managers are likely also to find that their own work will alter out of all recognition. Staff responsible to them will have different tasks, different skills and abilities, changed responsibility levels (higher or lower) and may well respond better to a different style of management. Staff are also more likely to be unionised and more aware of the possibilities for influencing management decisions. Additionally the manager will have the opportunity to use microelectronics directly to improve the quality and speed of information available to him and as a direct aid to better decision-making.

Changes are already evident in the way managers work in organisations where computers are extensively utilised. In many situations sales managers are able to get immediate access to the latest sales and stock information. Production managers can check the progress in assembly operations, supply problems, etc., and use the information to make decisions such as resource redeployment. Simulation models aid finance managers in making investment decisions. These and other developments will become common practice.

4

Office managers, systems specialists, methods advisors — in fact all those involved in performing or designing office work and training office staff — will become involved with the new office technology at some stage. Once the new microelectronic equipment is readily accessible, new applications will be identified, designed and installed. Many managers will find that an increasingly important aspect of their job will be to identify these new applications and manage their implementation.

## The nature of office work

Despite all these developments we believe that the basic nature and purpose of office work has not changed. There is still a requirement for letters and telexes, for telephone calls and cables, for orders and invoices, for reports and contracts, in fact for an apparently ever-increasing quantity of internal and external communications. Information of all kinds is received and processed, stored and retrieved. The function of the office is to contribute to the effectiveness of the total organisation, whether this is manufacturing, sales, or a professional or advisory service. However, if the purpose of the work has not changed, then the same cannot be said about the methods of handling the tasks that comprise office work. In the remainder of this chapter we look at some of these tasks and the impact of new technology on them and on the people who perform them.

*Accounting tasks*

Long gone are the days when every clerk used pens and pencils to scribe neatly in vast ledgers. Over the past twenty years the computer has absorbed more and more of such routine clerical tasks. Whether using mainframe computers of high capacity, computer bureaux or perhaps mini- or microcomputers, organisations have had to change clerical procedures in order to accommodate the new technology. This is especially true in the accounting function. Transactions can now be recorded on the computer by processing through keypunch or some other data conversion system, so that machine operators with no knowledge of accounting convert written or printed data into a form suitable for computer processing. With more sophisticated equipment even data conversion can be avoided with automatic recording taking place at the point of sale.

Many clerks can now communicate directly with the computer through a terminal or visual display unit sitting on the office desk; this feature is becoming increasingly common. By 'keying in' appropriate instructions, the clerk can call information such as customer details to the screen and then, again by depressing keys as if typing, can record transactions such as payments, product or sales details directly on to the computer. Interrogation facilities are also often available enabling clerks to seek out answers to queries that arise. Clerks involved in this kind of work, rather than acting simply as machine operators, must understand the basis of the systems and the transactions being undertaken. They must be able to read and interpret the information that is readily available and accessible via the keyboard and screen. When staff are familiar with the systems and their potential applications this type of man-machine interaction can add considerably to the interest of the work and in turn contribute to greater accuracy and productivity. At the same time, it raises questions about audit controls, about responsibility and authority levels, about the status and career implications especially where the work has a professional orientation, for example, in accountancy. Managers involved in the introduction of direct computer access by clerical staff will need to consider issues of these kinds both from the organisation's viewpoint as well as from the standpoint of individual employees and ensure that they are resolved to the satisfaction of both parties in order that the progress into the technological age in the office can proceed smoothly.

*Word processing*

In most organisations preparation of written communications, for example, letters and reports, forms a major part of office work. This is a process that is increasingly being automated with microprocessing technology. Dictating equipment, either individual pocket machines or central systems, including those using the internal telephone network, are frequently used in preference to face-to-face dictation, which is being abandoned in many organisations for cost reasons. Dictating systems combine effectively with another new piece of office equipment, the word processor. The latter is replacing the typewriter in some offices; its adaptability, wide range of applicability and the possibility of communicating between two or more word processors by linking them over telephone lines, gives rise to some of the more far-reaching predictions about the future of office work.

Word processors vary considerably in sophistication, in the range of special facilities they offer and in their capacity to handle large volumes of work. However, they all consist basically of the five main components illustrated and described in Exhibit 2. At the simplest level, word processors allow text to be created, stored in the 'memory' and retrieved for amendment or rearrangement. Alternatively, it can be combined with other information (perhaps stored on another memory disk) to create a completely new document. Although the original text is usually created by typing on a keyboard which forms part of the word processor, other options are available. For example, any preprinted text can be converted into suitable input for a word processor by means of an

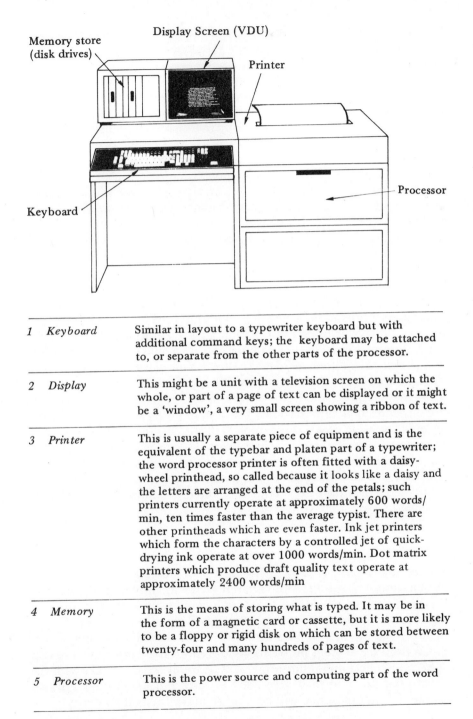

Memory store
(disk drives)

Display Screen (VDU)

Printer

Processor

Keyboard

| | | |
|---|---|---|
| 1 *Keyboard* | | Similar in layout to a typewriter keyboard but with additional command keys; the keyboard may be attached to, or separate from the other parts of the processor. |
| 2 *Display* | | This might be a unit with a television screen on which the whole, or part of a page of text can be displayed or it might be a 'window', a very small screen showing a ribbon of text. |
| 3 *Printer* | | This is usually a separate piece of equipment and is the equivalent of the typebar and platen part of a typewriter; the word processor printer is often fitted with a daisy-wheel printhead, so called because it looks like a daisy and the letters are arranged at the end of the petals; such printers currently operate at approximately 600 words/min, ten times faster than the average typist. There are other printheads which are even faster. Ink jet printers which form the characters by a controlled jet of quick-drying ink operate at over 1000 words/min. Dot matrix printers which produce draft quality text operate at approximately 2400 words/min |
| 4 *Memory* | | This is the means of storing what is typed. It may be in the form of a magnetic card or cassette, but it is more likely to be a floppy or rigid disk on which can be stored between twenty-four and many hundreds of pages of text. |
| 5 *Processor* | | This is the power source and computing part of the word processor. |

**EXHIBIT 2**   The main components of a word processor

optical character reader. This equipment can 'read' text and convert it to a form suitable for storage and subsequent printing via a word processor or computer.

The development of word processing obviously has enormous implications for those involved in document preparation. Typists and secretaries will have to acquire new skills. There is also a trend towards the separation of typing and administrative duties so that in future there may be different occupations, i.e. word processing operators and administrative secretaries. Differences will exist in the skills, abilities and aptitudes needed by staff in the two occupations.

It is frequently forecast that word processors will increase productivity and as a result reduce the number of typing jobs. However, at present in the UK this does not appear to be the result. In many organisations the same number of typists are employed but working for more document authors including new users. Whilst there has been an increase in productivity there has been little reduction in the number of jobs. It seems that operators, on becoming familiar with new equipment, are able to offer a wider range of services and in consequence expand their total job. Without word processors, however, the inevitable conclusion must be that if these additional services were available and utilised the new volume of work would result in more jobs.

If document authors are to make effective use of word processing they need to appreciate the potential and limitations of the new facilities. This may require them to modify their ways of working. Some organisations now find that they are able to justify word processing on account of time saved by senior staff rather than by savings on secretaries. Simple ways in which word processors help authors save time include the preparation of letters and reports with the aid of standard text and the facility to highlight changes in drafts so that the author does not have to reread the whole document whenever it is amended.

*Voice input*

Future developments may bring still more changes for document authors and typing staff. Although research is already well advanced in the development of systems that can generate 'printed' output using signals directly from the human voice, it is likely to be a number of years before voice input is commercially viable for normal correspondence. Apart from the obvious implications for typists, these sytems will have a substantial effect on authors; they will be required to interact with the word processor and they may need to further develop their skills in dictating, although they will be able to make corrections easily.

## Communicating printers

Word processors can now be linked over telephone lines either to other word processors or to compatible computers. As a result, text produced in one location can be printed elsewhere. At present in the UK this facility is used mainly for internal communications between distant locations in an organisation but elsewhere, in the USA, for example, word processors communicate between organisations. This has been made possible by the integration of the two major technical innovations, microelectronics and telecommunications. It has provided enormous potential for change in the way organisations operate internally as well as how they interact with customers and suppliers. In particular, the potential impact on the way office work is organised is considerable since it becomes both feasible and cost-effective under certain circumstances to disperse office activities. This in turn would have an effect on the numbers of staff engaged and their location. One consequence may be that organisations will have written work typed at one location where word processing staff are plentiful and printed at other locations where such staff are in short supply but where authors or recipients are based. Alternatively, for internal communications it may be possible to dispense with hard copy correspondence altogether and to send communications over telephone lines between screens and then to only print out a hard copy when the the recipient feels it necessary.

## Filing systems

Once text or other data has been entered into the type of system outlined earlier, it is available for long-term storage. Electronic filing and retrieval of information then becomes totally feasible. Retrieval may be in the original format, or alternatively in a format or sequence stipulated by the person interrogating the system.

When electronic mail is generally in use, computerised information storage, in preference to hard copy, is likely for several reasons. Whilst there is a mixture of hard copy and computer-held information, the hard copy must always be converted since computer files must be complete for it to be possible to efficiently employ data retrieval systems. Already, large blocks of information like *Hansard*, the record of each day's proceedings in the Houses of Parliament, can be kept on computer files. The advantage here, apart from the saving on traditional file storage space and filing staff, is that classification is usually handled at the time of retrieval rather than when the information is stored. This means that there is no danger of misfiling and documents that need cross-referencing can be stored once but accessed easily by the computer, using many different 'key words'.

Using computers as file storage media has been possible for a number of years, but it takes a great deal of computer memory as well as capacity for retrieval routines and until recently cost and size of computer memory made this non-viable. As computer components are reduced in size and become cheaper, whilst offering larger capacity for memory stores than ever before, computer filing becomes a realistic proposition. Once it is available and every manager has a visual display screen on which to summon any document for immediate reference, paper filing, for so long one of the most essential but least popular jobs in the office, will become redundant. The computer will handle the process much faster and with greater accuracy.

### Information bases

Apart from an organisation's own files, managers through their information departments generally have access to reference or specialist libraries and directories. Central systems are increasingly available via telephone links for reference through visual display screens. Viewdata services, such as Prestel and Oracle in the UK, are becoming widely available. World-wide literature-searching facilities are already extensively used in libraries and information departments. Subscription services of this kind will expand more as increasing demands are placed on them. In France, for example, the telephone directory is shortly to be made available for private telephone subscribers as well as business users, via a screen. This development is likely to create further business as users demand more information from the new facility.

### Electronic mail

Electronic mail is a more systematised means of distributing messages than just communications between printers. A comprehensive system of addressing messages is an integral part of an electronic mail system and items are usually channelled through a control point. At the present time those electronic mail systems which exist in the UK operate on a subscriber basis.

## Generations of office equipment

We have described some of the more recent technological innovations appearing in general offices. There are many other developments, particularly for specialist office functions. However, it would be unrealistic if we suggested that all offices already have a use for all the various devices or that the demand for a wider range of equipment will increase at a steady, even rate. Equipment and methods of an earlier technological era are likely to continue in use in many offices alongside some of the most advanced aids to office work. Although it can be argued

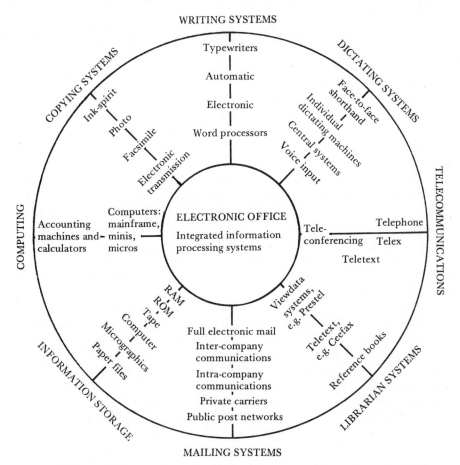

WRITING SYSTEMS

COPYING SYSTEMS

DICTATING SYSTEMS

Typewriters
Automatic
Electronic
Word processors

Ink-spirit
Photo
Facsimile
Electronic transmission

Face-to-face shorthand
Individual dictating machines
Central systems
Voice input

COMPUTING

TELECOMMUNICATIONS

Accounting machines and calculators
Computers: mainframe, minis, micros

ELECTRONIC OFFICE
Integrated information processing systems

Tele-conferencing
Telephone
Telex
Teletext

RAM
ROM
Tape
Computer
Micrographics
Paper files

Viewdata systems, e.g. Prestel
Teletext, e.g. Ceefax
Reference books

INFORMATION STORAGE

LIBRARIAN SYSTEMS

Full electronic mail
Inter-company communications
Intra-company communications
Private carriers
Public post networks

MAILING SYSTEMS

**EXHIBIT 3** The development of office systems. Note that none of the system lines, the spokes of the wheel, are separate and distinct. Most have a degree of overlap. The aim, however, is for all systems to be compatible and so able to communicate.

that the microprocessor, the essential component of many of the new systems, is a revolutionary invention bringing change at an unprecedented rate, it is also evident from an examination of developments in the nature of office work that changes follow a gradual, evolutionary process.

Exhibit 3 shows the development of office technology as a wheel. Each of the spokes of this wheel represents a different type of office task, one being concerned with writing systems, another with dictating, others with mailing, filing, computing, copying systems, and so on. Each spoke is shown as being independent and yet it is possible, with the convergence of the microprocessing and telecommunications techologies, to obtain maximum benefit for an organisation by designing an integrated system. Obviously, apart from providing benefits in the context of work method, this is also likely to offer benefits in terms of total cost. However, whilst an organisation might prefer to choose a sophisticated, fully integrated system, in practice, at any one time most organisations use equipment of several different generations on the same spoke of the wheel, as well as different generations of equipment from different spokes of the wheel. For example, typists using conventional typewriters can be found in many offices alongside clerks using visual display units which give them direct access to a central computer. In other situations, word processors are used widely and yet the mailroom is run on conventional lines with sorting of post by hand.

## Long-term planning

An important need for those reviewing the potential use of microelectronics, as well as those involved in the introduction of new office technology, is an awareness of the present stage of development within their own organisation: the type of equipment used and numbers employed, communications patterns and loadings, and the total information needs and means by which they are met. Then it is necessary to take a long-term view of communications and information processing in its broadest context. In this way it is possible for an organisation to make long-term plans for its office function. Equipment can be chosen not only to meet the needs of today but also integrated into a long-term plan aimed at meeting future requirements. For example, if the long-term plan is for several separate locations to communicate via the telecommunications network, then the organisation will need to ensure that any word processors that are purchased for separate locations are in fact capable of communicating and are compatible with each other. Whilst this appears to be obvious, in large organisations operating on a decentralised basis without a central buying function or a central point for advice on methods and equipment, the number of different manufacturers supplying office equipment can be considerable and, to date, equipment purchased from different manufacturers is seldom able to communicate without specially designed conversion equipment.

Any long-term plan should also highlight changes in staff requirements. For example, the organisation may decide that in future fewer shorthand typists will be required but there will be a need for more clerical staff capable of handling responsible work with a high level of decision-making. A knowledge of the skill patterns and numbers required for the different types of work in the future is likely to influence today's recruitment.

Staff who have been doing some of the more routine kinds of office work, collating and checking data for example, or straightforward copy typing, will need careful training if they are to cope with the demands of the new equipment. Some may find the challenge too demanding and will need to be trained for quite different types of work. Managers will want to anticipate and plan for situations of this kind and some examples of the issues which can occur appear later in the case studies. Long-term planning includes the development of a strategy for coping with change but in the case studies we describe several situations where managers had to adapt to change with little opportunity to plan strategies at an early stage and foresee the problems.

One thing remains undoubtedly true; many office managers will have to cope with wide-ranging changes over the next decade. From further reference to Exhibit 3 it can be seen that change is likely on more than one dimension or spoke. Change in the office is a continuous process and this in itself is not a new situation for office managers, and their staff or their advisers. However, the difference in the future is that the rate of change will be much greater than any which has gone before. Also the rate of change will not be altogether under the direct control of individual organisations and, therefore, of its managers.

To meet competition at home and overseas it is essential that the office plays its part in achieving cost-effective operations by providing essential information for management. New developments in telecommunications are already far advanced in the USA, Japan and in Europe. In the UK it is planned to improve telecommunications facilities dramatically over the next five years. As these facilities improve so the effect will be to encourage existing users to extend their range of telecommunications facilities and, in turn, for more organisations to investigate wide applications of new office technologies. Competition as always will be the spur to progress and office staff and their managers will be required to adapt to the new working methods.

---

### SUMMARY POINTS

1 Office equipment and systems have been evolving for many years but now, with the development of the silicon chip and microprocessing techniques, the rate of change is expected to increase dramatically.

2 For several years to come the new systems will exist side by side with the equipment from an earlier era. This may pose equipment compatibility problems and delay the development of advanced inter-organisation communication facilities, e.g. electronic mail.

3 Organisations, however, will be able to benefit individually from innovations in text and data processing. For optimum equipment utilisation, new working methods will have to be introduced for managers and professional staff as well as for clerks and secretaries. There will be a need to integrate a variety of different functions and skills.

4 A considerable amount of training associated with the new technology will be required at both the awareness and operational levels. This will require commitment from managers if implementation is to go ahead smoothly.

5 Managers should develop a long-term plan for communications media and information systems with regard to equipment and to staff. The wheel, presented again here, can be used to assist in identifying the type of equipment in current use in the organisation and for plotting the longer-term equipment plan. This should be linked to the associated financial, manpower and training plans.

ACTION:
1    Circle equipment already in use
2    Box intended next steps

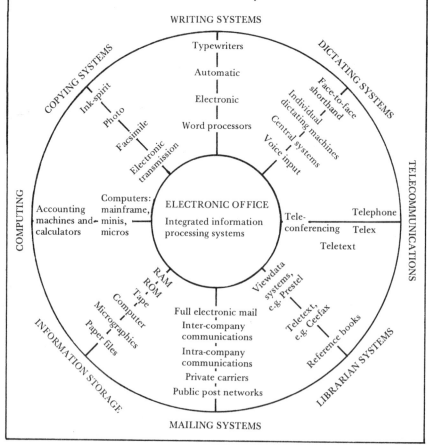

# CHAPTER 2

# The changing nature of office work

In Chapter 1 we looked at some of the developments in office technology that have created opportunities for radical change in the way office work is carried out. However, it is clear from a cursory glance at modern offices that the availability of new equipment is not sufficient, in itself, to ensure its rapid introduction on a wide scale. Many factors — economic, social and political — influence the rate of change. Some of these factors will be discussed in this chapter. In the first part of the chapter we will consider the tasks, roles and status of office employees, especially clerical staff, and how these have developed. This will enable us to identify trends and factors influencing the rate of change in the 1980s.

## Work in the office

The office has been described as 'the nerve centre' of an organisation. It provides the co-ordinating and processing function for all the information flows in and out of the organisation as well as internally. Office work is performed in all employment sectors, both public and private. Whilst office work is highly concentrated in the service industries, e.g. banking, insurance and public utilities, there are also office staff in manufacturing and other industries where they provide a support function. Many terms and classifications have been used to describe those working in offices, e.g. non-manual, salaried, black-coated and white-collared. The terminology varies between countries, but the fact that such terms exist suggests distinctions between manual and non-manual work in most industrialised countries. Such distinctions remain, even though many manual workers in automated manufacturing situations perform few manual tasks whereas typists and VDU operators may carry out tasks mostly manual in nature.

Clerical and secretarial tasks have changed considerably during this century. In more recent times, work methods and functions such as

15

finance and accounts, customer records, personnel records and production control have changed beyond recognition in many organisations because of the widespread use of mainframe computers Prior to this revolution, other technological changes had an impact upon the nature of office work and the skills required, amongst them the use of mechanical and electronic calculators and electric typewriters. Each of these innovations offered improved facilities to the organisation whilst at the same time requiring those working as clerks and secretaries to adapt to new working methods and practices in order for the full potential to be materialised. New roles have been created in organisations to cope with the problems of designing systems to take full advantage of the opportunities offered by this new and more expensive equipment, e.g. Organisation and Methods (O&M) specialists and systems designers.

Focusing upon the nature of the clerk's work, one feature of more recent developments such as computerisation has been the extent to which control of the processes has been taken from the clerk and transferred to the machine. Whilst earlier changes mechanised certain discrete office routines as illustrated by the use of calculators, use of this equipment still left the control with the clerk. This type of equipment was an aid to the clerk in performing his tasks. Early applications of computers, however, were not as an aid to the clerk but resulted in a questionning of the appropriateness of traditional clerical systems. Computerisation, then, resulted in large parts of the administrative and clerical functions in organisations being automated. As a result systems have been designed such that the lower level of decision-making has been built into the computer. Consequently, control over work has been transferred from clerks to computers. The machine has also taken over certain of the skills formerly demanded of clerks, such as a high level of numeracy and the ability to spot discrepancies and misplaced entries. Such changes in the nature of work, in turn, have had an impact on the status of the clerk both within the organisation itself and in the world outside work.

Nevertheless, even today, when a manual worker moves to a white-collar job he often feels and acts as if he has moved from one social class to another. Whilst the prestige of his new job generally may be no greater than his old one, normally he will consider it to be greater and a rise in status resulting from personal merit. Traditionally, white-collar employees have undoubtedly enjoyed higher social, occupational and economic status, and their role and prestige, their rights and duties have, in the past, also differentiated them in their work environment from manual workers. This differentiation has extended to life outside work — to the employee's home and family. However, as indicated earlier, as a result of mechanisation and automation, work performed in the office has tended to decline generally in intellectual demands and this in turn has made such work accessible to wider sections of the working population. Additionally, the larger proportion of white-collar workers in the working population as a whole, the less elitist is the group. This decline in exclusiveness has been accompanied by a reduction in relative earnings to the point where there is a large degree of overlap between the earnings of skilled manual workers and salaried personnel.

Whilst the status of general clerks has declined over a long period the new occupations associated with the transfer of clerical work to computers, i.e. systems design and computer programming, have, attracted a high status. As further new technologies become available with more sophisticated software, the increased simplicity of programming computers could facilitate the transfer back to clerical work of some lower-level decision-making. Choices will be available to the equipment purchasers and to the systems designers about the degree of discretion afforded clerical workers. The outcome of these decisions will influence the future status of clerical staff generally. As well as having an impact on the wider social structure, in turn these changes will have a bearing at the individual level where expectations of work may remain unfulfilled.

Detailed statistics about numbers employed specifically in office work are not generally available although relevant data are published in sources such as the UK's *Department of Employment Gazette*. As an indication of the numbers engaged in clerical-type work in Great Britain* in 1978, well over a quarter of those employed in manufacturing industries were engaged in clerical, administrative and technical occupations. To this must be added the very much higher percentage of the total involved in clerical work in service industries particularly banking, insurance and finance, as well as central and local government. (See *Central Statistical Office Abstract of Statistics 1980,* Table 6.4.)

It is clear that in countries such as the UK industrialisation and the subsequent economic changes have been accompanied by a shift to white-collar employment and to the service industries in particular. This is illustrated in Exhibit 4 which shows the trend in employment in service industries. It has been calculated that 75 million people currently employed in the service industries in Western Europe, Canada, USA and Japan would have been working in industry and agriculture if the distribution of labour at the turn of this century had remained the same. An accompanying trend has been in the composition of the labour force, where an increasing proportion of females have been employed. As an illustration, in Great Britain as recently as 1931 there were still slightly more men then women doing office work. By 1961 women constituted nearly two-thirds of the office

*Great Britain includes England, Scotland and Wales. The United Kingdom includes England, Scotland, Wales and Northern Ireland.

**Earliest record**

| | Earliest record Date | Earliest record % A | c. 1900 B | c. 1939 C | c. 1950 D | c. 1958 E | c. 1969 F | 1970-75 G | Change in proportion 1900-75 1% | Representing persons in 1975, 000s |
|---|---|---|---|---|---|---|---|---|---|---|
| Austria | 1870 | 24 | 31 | | 29.8 | 34.4 | 39.7 | 45.2 | 14 | 425 |
| Belgium | 1880 | 36 | 39.4 | 35.2 | 36.7 | 44.6 | 50.0 | 55.6 | 16 | 640 |
| Denmark | 1870 | 22 | 30 | 40.3 | 42.8 | 44.2 | 49.6 | 57.3 | 27 | 670 |
| Finland | 1880 | 12 | 13 | 18.0 | 25.3 | 30.4 | 40.8 | 47.1 | 34 | 760 |
| France | 1845 | 20 | 24.9 | 33.5 | 36.5 | 37.3 | 44.4 | 45.6 | 21 | 4,335 |
| West Germany | 1882 | 22 | 25.6 | 32.5 | 32.5 | 36.7 | 41.3 | 44.6 | 19 | 5,175 |
| Greece | | | | | | 27.0 | 28.6 | 31.5 | | (400)* |
| Iceland | | | | | 31.1 | 42.4 | 43.9 | | | |
| Ireland (Eire) | 1841 | 14.3 | 27.8 | 34.1 | 35.3 | 38.7 | 41.9 | 42.9 | 15 | 170 |
| Italy | 1870 | 15 | 21.1 | 22.9 | 25.7 | 28.4 | 32.6 | 40.5 | 19 | 3,690 |
| Netherlands | 1849 | 25 | 35.6 | 40.6 | 41.7 | 45.5 | 50.8 | | 15 | 600 |
| Norway | 1875 | 27 | 31.4 | 38.9 | 37.3 | 41.4 | 48.5 | 55.3 | 24 | 405 |
| Portugal | | | | 26.4 | 26.5 | 27.7 | 33.0 | 32.3 | | (400)* |
| Spain | 1877 | 14 | 19 | | 24.9 | 25.7 | 32.2 | 39.8 | 21 | 2,800 |
| Sweden | 1840 | 10 | 19 | 34.8 | | 43.4 | 50.9 | 56.3 | 37 | 1,465 |
| Switzerland | 1860 | 13 | 25.4 | 32.9 | | 38.6 | 40.0 | 44.0 | 19 | 570 |
| Turkey | | | | 9.9 | 8.9 | 10.2 | 14.4 | 19.0 | | (1,500)* |
| United Kingdom (GB) | 1840 | 33 | 37 | 48.0 | 33.0 | 39.3 | 41.2 | 52.4 | 15 | 3,750 |
| Canada | 1880 | 19 | 28.9 | 36.3 | 44.0 | 50.4 | 59.6 | 63.8 | 35 | 3,535 |
| USA | 1820 | 15.3 | 34.6 | 46.3 | 49.6 | 57.5 | 61.7 | 61.2 | 27 | 27,175 |
| Japan | 1872 | 10.2 | 15.3 | 21.8 | | 39.6 | 46.2 | 50.0 | 35 | 18,460 |

*Approx. total* 75,000

*Estimated

**EXHIBIT 4**  Employment in service industries as a percentage of total employment. *Source:* Pollard, S., 'The rise of the service industries and white-collar employment', *in* Gustafsson, B. (Editor), *Post-industrial Society*, Croom Helm, London (1979).

labour force with 2 million women working in offices compared with 600,000 in 1931. Over 70 per cent of the increase in the total female labour force during the period went into office work. In constrast only 13 per cent of the increase in the male labour force entered office employment. During the same period the total labour force increased 25 per cent, office employment 130 per cent, with the employment of female office staff 216 per cent. Many reasons have been given for this trend in industrialised societies towards white-collar employment, particularly in the service sector. The increasing size and complexity of organisations, business and social, seems to create the need for increased degrees of co-ordination and control. Mass production has made technological development economically feasible in manufacturing processes hence considerably increasing the output of goods. Technological developments in the office may have been slower, hence the relative increase in office employment. Also, increasing affluence in society tends to lead to more emphasis being placed upon welfare provision and hence greater numbers employed in providing and administering services. Further it has also been suggested that Parkinson's law operates and bureaucracies will grow as a result of internal mechanisms irrespective of the needs of the organisation being administered. Much of the gain has been in the public sector and in voluntary and non-profit-making associations where it is argued that the budgetary procedures fail to curb 'empire-building' and competition is non-existent. Further, personal assistants and additional secretaries may be a means by which successful executives can be rewarded as an alternative to higher salaries.

Whilst these explanations for the rapid growth in white-collar employment are rather contentious they do point us in the direction of possible causes. Nevertheless, despite both the attempts of governments and business to curb the expansion of white-collar employment and increasing mechanisation and automation, historically the trend has been one of growth. What our data do not demonstrate is the trend in the various occupations classified as white-collar. It seems likely, particularly during periods of general economic difficulty as seen in the early 1980s, that attempts to curb the increase will affect some sections more than others. Such attempts at constraint may lead to a redistribution of work amongst staff and even occupational groups. These changes may create greater opportunities for interesting work for some staff but inevitably there will be others who will not be able to cope with the new demands and pressures.

The existence of a new technology does not, of itself, bring about change. This point is illustrated by considering the adoption of computers. Whilst computers were developed in the 1940s largely for scientific purposes it was not until the mid- to late-1960s that computer manufacturers started to make organisations aware of their capability for wider use and computers then began significantly to penetrate the office. Even in the early 1980s many organisations still function competitively without the aid of computers. This example of the rate of adoption of new technology serves to remind us that technical feasibility alone will not lead to widespread adoption. Alternatives have to be economically viable and socially and politically acceptable for change to be introduced and it is to the consideration of these factors that we now turn.

## The economics of office automation

As mentioned in Chapter 1, the new equipment is becoming an increasingly viable economic proposition for a greater number of organisations, medium and small in size as well as the large multi-nationals and the public sector authorities. Once generally available the cost of the equipment falls very rapidly. For example, calculators can be purchased in a chain store today for around one tenth of the price five years ago. Similarly, with writing systems, the difference in cost between a very sophisticated electronic machine at the bottom end of the word processing scale and an ordinary electric typewriter is no more than about 20 per cent. The comparable electronic machine has the advantages of relying on fewer moving parts so there is less to maintain, on being faster and more versatile and of giving superior quality. These factors make their introduction more attractive. Additionally, in many cases, especially those where more sophisticated equipment is used, the software can be programmed to meet the user's precise requirements.

In terms of cost saving, a factor often overlooked when considering the viability of new equipment is the cost of floor space. Where the rental cost per square metre of office space is high, as in London and other major cities, new technology can offer substantial savings on this factor alone, especially when it is applied to reducing space for filing systems. For some organisations the need to economise on the cost of space is of even more importance than saving on staff. Employees are productive; files are mostly a non-productive investment.

Most organisations, however, tend to quote a saving in labour costs as part of the economic justificaiton for office technology. This seems rarely to be achieved, for reasons outlined earlier, but it may be that as a result of the changes employers are better able to find employees with appropriate skills. Even in times of high unemployment there continues to be a shortage of office staff in some large connurbations and some organisations may invest in new office technology because of the high cost of attracting and keeping suitable staff.

On the macro scale, the need to match competitors in terms of performance and cost will encourage organisations to look for ways of improving productivity and using the office more effectively as an information resource. There is likely to be a 'push-pull' effect; countries such as the USA, Japan and Germany already make proportionately greater use of new office technology than other countries who will have to change in order to compete in world-wide markets. Apart from any central initiatives from governments or other interest groups, the adoption of office technology on a large scale by the multinational companies will no doubt have an effect on the practices and work styles of their suppliers and customers. An example of the 'push-pull' effect occurred with regard to the introduction of direct-debiting to a customer's bank account for goods supplied rather than waiting for payment on presentation of an invoice in the normal way. This practice, which was first favoured by the large corporations, is now also used by smaller businesses for goods delivered to industry and to the general public.

These then are some of the economic factors that influence decision-makers towards investment in office technology; availability and reliability, cost-saving potential and the need to remain competitive. Economic factors working against the introduction of new technology include the difficulty some organisations have in proving that it is cost-effective and will produce an adequate return on investment. Traditionally, there has been very limited investment in office technology and methodologies for measuring costs accurately and assessing cost-effectiveness are consequently not well developed.

Difficulties and instability in the market place will doubtless lead managers to be cautious about making a significant investment in their offices. Nevertheless, eventually they may see little alternative. The real limitations possibly lie outside their control. These include the ability of telecommunications networks to cope with the increasing demands as the use of communicating microtechnology expands, as well as the successful agreement between networks to allow free flow of communication over public lines across the globe.

A 1979 survey by Input, an international consultancy, showed that the major obstacle to the introduction of office technology was resistance to change, both by managers and clerks and it is to social aspects of this kind that we now turn.


## Social and political factors influencing the adoption of office technology

Adoption of new office technology presents quite radical changes for office staff including management. Some of the changes are immediately apparent when comparing an office with traditional equipment and one with the most recent technology, e.g. VDU screens have replaced conventional typewriters, there are higher levels of audio-typing. The impact on the manager's job and how it is performed is less apparent.

Some staff find the prospect of working with 'television' screens instead of hard copy from typewriters or in ledgers very worrying. One of the main concerns expressed relates to the impact of continually operating a VDU upon health and safety, both in the short and long-term. There have been numerous investigations into the effects of working with screens upon eyesight and health more generally. Another concern that has been expressed relates to the stress for the operator resulting from working with the equipment. Whilst evidence is not as yet conclusive and in the main relates only to shorter-term problems, it would seem that previously healthy employees operating well designed equipment arranged well at the workplace are no more likely to suffer from health problems than those using the more conventional equipment. High levels of job satisfaction have been expressed by most staff investigated who are using such equipment. In some situations, however, arrangement of staff into word-processing centres seems to have encouraged a competitive approach between operators and the equipment. This could possibly prove to be stressful if continued over a long period. (The principles of good equipment and workplace design are discussed in Chapter 6.)

At a more senior level, the new office technology may contribute to the stress experienced by managers and others. Particularly in the short term, managers may feel that they have lost control over both staff and departmental activities. Uncertainty and anxiety is often generated where changes of any kind are being introduced. In the office, however, these changes are likely to be of greater concern because they are likely to have such a radical impact on the total operation.

The perception held by many managers of a loss of control over the work of staff possibly results from an inability to observe and physically monitor work completed as well as the possiblity of interference with the systems and uncertainties about the level of security. Much of this anxiety results from a lack of knowledge both about the equipment and the software, i.e. the systems design and operation. For example, many systems can closely monitor their own use and work carried out by staff. Anxiety amongst senior staff, as amongst clerks and secretaries, can be reduced by involving them in equipment trails to encourage familiarisation. For example, in an insurance company, two word processors were installed on a trial basis and two secretaries were given basic training. After two months, however, most of the typists in the area had taught themselves the basics and one of the company directors was able to type his own work on occasions. The machines, installed in a relaxed way, had sold themselves to the people who would use them. The familiarisation which comes from trial experimentation was also encouraged in a chemical company where it was possible for some staff on occasions to borrow microcomputers for use at home. Whilst freedom of this kind may be beyond the scope of most organisations, the philosophy behind it is surely not. It recognises that people may need the reassurance of private play as well as careful training in order to encourage them to take 'ownership' of a major new tool of working life. Also by developing this familiarity with the equipment and its capability, managers, specialists and staff will identify new applications for the equipment.

Many educational institutions at all levels are beginning to use more technological aids to learning and this will increase the receptivity and expectations of young people with regard to office technology. The availability of computer games and home equipment such as video machines and even sewing machines which are controlled by microprocessors, has the effect of making people more 'machine-minded' — an attribute frequently required by those selecting staff to work with new technology. Therefore, resistance to microtechnology on the grounds of fear of the equipment can be expected to diminish over time.

Another major concern, however, particularly to governments and trade unions, is unlikely to be resolved so easily. This is the effect of office technology on the total number of jobs, especially office jobs. During periods when unemployment is rising both nationally and internationally it is to be expected that concern will be expressed about potential job losses resulting from the adoption of new technologies. In many countries, high-level discussions are taking place involving government, employer's groups and trade unions with the aim of formulating policies. Many trade unions representing office workers have prepared reports to advise and guide members. In the UK, unions such as APEX (the Association of Professional, Executive, Clerical and Computer Staff) and ASTMS (the Association of Scientific, Technical and Managerial Staff) as well as the TUC (Trades Union Congress) have identified the benefits to be derived from the adoption of new technology. However, they have highlighted the need for safeguards to employment such as a movement towards a shorter working week as well as the negotiation within organisations of 'Technology Agreements' to protect the interests of staff. In the UK and elsewhere, following on from technology agreements, office managers may find themselves involved in negotiations with trade unions for the first time. This is likely particularly where, by tradition, there has been a comparatively low level of formal organisation amongst office staff and negotiations have been limited to organisation-wide issues. Even where internal staff associations represent staff, the models for consultation recommended by trade unions may well be adopted. These are discussed in Chapter 8, where we consider technology agreements and the planning of change.

## Introducing change in the office

It has been suggested that organisations consist of four important interacting variables.* These four variables are shown in Exhibit 5. Organisations, whether in the overall sense or at the level of the office, have *tasks* to be performed. *Technology*, in the form of equipment, aids performance of the task but may at the same time restrict the choice of method for carrying out the task or the task itself. In this context *structure* is the system of authority, workflow, information systems, co-ordination and communication. *People* make up the staff in the organisation. These individuals have expectations from work and their attitudes and actions will determine the success of the organisation. Clearly individual attitudes and expectations change in relation to work during the individual's working life. These changes are the result of complex interactions between both work-related factors and their wider social experiences.

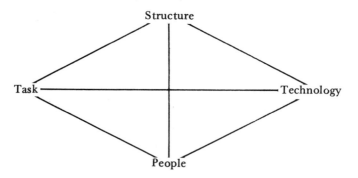

**EXHIBIT 5** Interdependent variables in the organisation

These four variables are highly interdependent so that a change in one will almost certainly elicit a change in the others. Consequently, one would anticipate that changes in technology would influence the pattern of relationships in the office. Changes in technology may also lead to questioning of the structure and influence structural changes. People's attitudes and expectations, in turn, may be shaped by changes on the other dimensions. An important consideration when planning change is which of the four variables most readily lends itself to manipulation and control.

Automation in the office will be successfully implemented only where the consent and acceptance of all interested parties is gained. One of the key tasks of managers responsible for implementing change will be to

*For more information see Leavitt, H.J., 'Applied organizational change in industry; structural, technological and humanistic approaches', *in* March, J.G. (Editor), *Handbook of Organizations*, Rand McNally (1965).

achieve such agreement. In such circumstances, the manager's task should include an assessment of how the system operates, identification of variances from the goals being sought, isolation of causes and initiation of corrective action. Where the aim is the introduction of new technology the manager should consider implications in terms of tasks, structure and people and identify acceptable solutions.

In many cases the introduction of large computer systems has occupied years rather than months. During this period the organisation must continue functioning. Consequently, earlier traditional and new systems may have to be operated in parallel. This can place considerable strain on the staff involved. In such circumstances, attention is often focused on the immediate but temporary problems at a time when a broad perspective focusing on longer-term consequences is required.

During the discussion about technological change the parties involved, management and staff representatives, are unlikely to fully appreciate its impact. Consequently, the new structures created may later fail to satisfy those staff employed on the task and the new tasks associated with the technological changes may not meet staff expectations. On the other hand, staff may be disappointed by the slow response of management to implement new technologies which would aid them in performing their work. Discrepancies of this nature between expectations and experiences may result in decisions by the individuals concerned to mimimise contribution to the enterprise or leave altogether. Such responses may be individual or collective but they are often dysfunctional for the organisation since they interfere with the overall performance of the office and do not help those managers requiring the information for decision-making purposes.

Earlier in this chapter we noted that over many years the relative status of the clerk has declined. Some of the tasks associated with the new technologies are likely to be less skilled, more routine and machine-controlled and lower in authority and responsibility. The skills required at lower levels in the office are predominantly manual rather than intellectual and opportunities for advancement to higher organisational levels very limited. Technological change, if adopted, could continue the trend. On the other hand, in some situations, office technology may actually increase the demands made on office staff. In the following chapters we aim to demonstrate that viable alternatives exist in the design of work systems to enable managers to create work that is rewarding and satisfying for the staff involved as well as efficient in organisational terms.

We believe that the challenge in carrying out work which is rewarding and satisfying in itself will contribute substantially to the effectiveness of staff working with new technology. This approach therefore offers real benefit to the manager.

## SUMMARY POINTS

1 Generally, there have been considerable changes in the nature of office work and a steady decline in the status of office staff. Office work traditionally has been regarded as of a higher status than manual work. Computerisation, however, eroded many of the skills and there has been a relative decline in the salaries of office staff compared to those of manual staff. Exceptions to this include the new technical office jobs such as systems design and computer programming.

2 Consideration of microelectronics applications in the office tends to highlight the important role of the office as the nerve centre of the organisation.

3 Savings on numbers employed may be the basis of cost justification for capital investment. Factors such as the reduction in filing space, labour-market competitiveness and overall business competitiveness should also be considered.

4 One major obstacle to the introduction of new office technology is said to be the resistance to change of managers and clerks.

5 The new technologies available could be applied in a way which would allow the growth of a small knowledge-based elite, some people having access to, and appreciation of, information whilst others are employed in more routine machine-feeding tasks.

6 In general, people in technologically advanced countries are becoming more used to operating sophisticated equipment, not only at work but during leisure time. Microprocessor-controlled tools and games are increasingly used at home and in education as well as at work.

7 When planning changes, the four inter-related variables — task, technology, structure and people — should be examined in turn to assess the impact of change in one dimension on the others.

# CHAPTER 3

# Improving performance and job satisfaction in the office

It is claimed that the successful implementation of technological change in the office can lead to considerable productivity improvements. This is the case particularly with word processing. One example which has received considerable publicity and seems fairly typical of the claims made was at the Bradford Metropolitan Council where a shared-logic word-processing system was introduced in the Directorate of Development in July 1977. The Council claimed that substantial benefits from the innovation came about: staff cut from 44 to 22; work load increased by 19 per cent; annual savings of £58,000 per annum.

Other studies of word-processing installations* have shown equally impressive productivity gains. In one recent survey of fourteen word-processing installations, including some of the largest and most established in the UK, managers in twelve cases reported reductions in typing and secretarial jobs of 3 to 75 per cent directly as a result of word processing. In each case productivity had improved, ranging from 10 to 300 per cent. The improvement in efficiency and the reduction of costs were the main reasons given for introducing the new technologies. In some instances organisations were experiencing difficulties in attracting and retaining suitably qualified personnel. Additionally, the high cost of city-centre office accommodation may have accelerated the changes.

The Bradford Metropolitan Council example of word processing would probably have not received as much attention if it had not been for subsequent events. The staff in this office, in common with other UK local government offices, are represented by NALGO, the National Association of Local Government Officers. Following the introduction of word processing a Bradford group of NALGO members formed an unofficial pressure group and issued a document criticising union

*For example, see McMahon, F., 'Office drudges and the bosses who can't spell', *Computing* (8 March 1980).

officials for the way in which they had handled the system's introduction. This group claimed that overall it was not in the best interests of members because of the job losses, job deskilling and likely staff alienation.

In the autumn of 1978, when the Council wished to extend shared-logic systems to other areas it approached NALGO. Following joint discussions the union held a secret ballot amongst 150 typists seeking views about the management proposals. These typists rejected the plans. Nevertheless, the management proceeded with its plans and instigated an O&M study in one division. Eighteen typists went on strike for two and a half weeks, a strike later made official by the union. A return to normal working was agreed on the basis that a tripartite working party comprising three of the community's elected councillors, three senior managers and three NALGO representatives, was set up. This working party was to consider the broader aspects of new technology.    This case serves to illustrate some of the problems being experienced in organisations attempting to introduce new office technology. Whilst an earlier project demonstrated the potential for productivity improvement, the changes aroused feelings amongst staff that both hindered and limited subsequent change. Another example of failure in implementation occurred in a British University*. Faulty word-processing equipment, poor training both of operators and users, together with an apparent lack of change management, contributed to an actual decrease in productivity. Word processing in this case was abandoned.

In many other cases the new technology has failed to meet early predictions of productivity improvement. In addition to the factors already mentioned (poor equipment selection and inadequate training, for example), organisations have failed to plan the change. Insufficient consideration has been given to alternative strategies for planning and implementation. The combination of these factors in many instances has let to higher costs in organisational and/or personal terms than would have been the case if more consideration had been given to these human aspects before embarking on the change.

Much of the debate about the impact of new technologies in the office has centred upon the effect upon overall employment levels and particularly women in employment. However, attention has been focused also on the jobs being created. Word processing is believed by many to lead to a reduction in typing skills, greater performance monitoring, a greater fragmentation of tasks, and health problems resulting from over-exposure to VDUs. Neither is this debate limited to academics and trade union leaders; it is increasingly being aired on television and in the popular press.

*Bird, E., *Information technology in the office; the impact on women's jobs*, UK Equal Opportunities Commission (1980).

Other contributions to the improvement of office efficiency come from both the systems designers and the O&M specialists. As in the case of management introducing new technologies, these specialists are being increasingly challenged to design systems that meet not only organisational objectives but also the needs of both job-holders and system users. These specialists depend upon the active co-operation of staff for their schemes to be successfully implemented. Frequently they are having to consider alternative strategies for design and implementation in order for their proposals to gain acceptance.

Following on from this illustration of the problems in introducing new technology in the office, and our own experiences, we believe that managers wishing to improve office productivity will have to increasingly consider these apects before selecting from available alternatives. Whilst technical and cost considerations associated with new technologies will remain of importance in decision-making, these other non-quantifiable aspects will also have to be taken note of. The questions of most concern, in this and the subsequent chapters, can be summarised as:

1    How can we design work systems more effectively?
2    What alternative ways are there of introducing change?
3    When are alternatives appropriate?
4    How can we alleviate problems of staff motivation resulting from poorly designed changes?

In this chapter we shall consider two questions in our list. First, we will look at organisational experimentation where the aims have been alleviation of motivational problems in the office. We will categorise these changes in order to establish alternative approaches. Our focus will be the actual jobs and the organisation of work. We have selected this focus because managers are often in a position to make changes to the structure of jobs and work organisation and, as we shall demonstrate, positive results can be achieved in terms of meeting both organisational goals and employee needs. However, we are not disregarding the importance of rewards, general personnel policies and practices, and the physical work environment in the creation and maintenance of staff morale. Whilst not our prime focus, reference is made to these factors in relation to staff motivation, particularly in the case material presented later.

We shall also examine these changes in organisation with a view to answering the second question, i.e. 'What alternative ways are there of introducing changes?'. We will report case examples using diffferent approaches and consider some of the particular problems and issues in implementing change.

The information provided in this chapter is based on an analysis of 34 case examples. We present the reasons for change, the nature of changes actually implemented, the way in which changes were introduced and the difficulties experienced. Whilst in most cases the implementation of new technology was not the focus, we believe that lessons can be learnt from these cases which have direct relevance to the problems of introducing change, including new technology.

## Reasons for change

Before considering the specific cases we should perhaps briefly reflect on the nature of motivational problems in the office. In many cases it is possible to identify a chain of events or circumstances that contribute to 'the problem'. Looking at Exhibit 6 we can see an illustration. In this imaginary case, low productivity is contributing to high levels of frustration which in turn contribute to low morale. The low morale in turn is influencing the decision to leave the job. As is often the case where there is high labour turnover the training resources are unable then to adequately prepare staff for the work. The clerks, finding difficulty in coping with the work, produce less. It is often the case that there is no readily identifiable starting point in the chain. In such a situation, the manager has to decide his main aims and reasons for making changes and then take action at the appropriate point in the chain.

In our survey we identified one or more reasons for making the changes in the 34 cases studied. We have summarised these reasons in

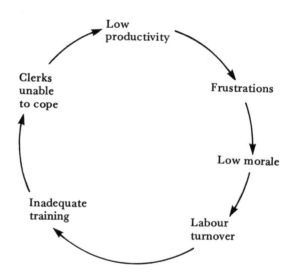

**EXHIBIT 6**  Motivational and operational problems: a chain of events and circumstances

| Reason | Frequency |
|---|---|
| Efficiency | 15 |
| Job satisfaction, morale, job interest | 10 |
| To create job opportunities | 4 |
| Labour turnover, unrest, labour attraction, absenteeism | 7 |
| Accompanying innovation | 4 |
| Organisational problems | 1 |
| More democratic style | 1 |
| Number of reasons | 42 |
| Number of cases | 34 |

**EXHIBIT 7**   Reasons stated for introducing changes to clerical or similar jobs

Exhibit 7. The principal reason for introducing changes to jobs and work organisation was to improve efficiency. In five cases increases in both efficiency and employee satisfaction were sought. In a total of ten instances employee satisfaction, morale or job interest were issues of concern. Technological innovation, including computerisation and word processing, was the stated reason for changing jobs and work organisation in four cases. In these reported experiments changes were often made following some form of automation or mechanisation. These changes, however, were often there for remedial purposes, to overcome problems created as a result of technological change. Only in four cases did job design and work organisation get consideration alongside the technological change.

## Changes in job design and work organisation

We have formed four categories of change. We will describe each with illustrations.

### 1   Job enlargement (1 case)

Job enlargement can be defined as the expansion of the job from a central task to include one or more additional and related tasks which are usually of a similar type. In the one case examined an attempt was made through the rationalisation of office work procedures to reduce costs and increase efficiency by 15 to 20 per cent. Inventory work had been split into two jobs: materials scheduling and materials expediting. Following change, some functions were computerised and the remaining tasks were combined so that the new job had a wider content than the original ones. The jobs, however, were still made up of tasks of similar types.

31

## 2   Job enrichment (13 cases)

This technique is usually applied in order to increase the motivational content of individual jobs by increasing opportunities within the job for employees to feel a sense of achievement and recognition. It generally means the delegation to staff of responsibilities normally carried out by the supervision or management. For example, staff may be made responsible for planning and control aspects essential for job performance.

In many of the 13 cases job changes resulted in staff having more contact with customers. Typically, clerks were assigned responsibility for specific customers (possibly on a geographical or alphabetical basis). Employees were required to identify themselves on work they processed and then to deal with any customer queries. This enabled clerks to correct their own errors. Clerks could also then handle customer enquiries. In two cases clerks had the opportunity of meeting customers on special occasions. Where the user of the service was in another department within the organisation the clerk was assigned the task of checking errors in the original documents directly with those previously involved. Clerks were made responsible for such aspects as letter writing and answering telephone queries.

In several cases jobs were combined in order to create a more demanding job, particularly where subdivision of the work led to the creation of highly repetitive tasks and inefficiencies in operation. As an example of subdivision of the work in one case seven clerks were required to process orders for spare parts. The work was organised so that one clerk acknowledged the order, one recorded it, two filled out the parts number, one filled in the official order forms and two handled despatch.

An important aspect of many of the job changes was to establish clear lines of authority. Job objectives were agreed and specific targets set. In one case as a result of computerisation a self-monitoring system of performance evaluation for employees was made possible.

Increased involvement in problem-solving was an important element of several job redesign exercises. Direct customer contact increased the employee's involvement in problem-solving activity — whether answering initial enquiries, or correcting errors. In one case bank employees were required to balance paid statements with remittances. The data generated then had to be translated into a form suitable for computer processing.

### AN EXAMPLE OF JOB ENRICHMENT

*Organisation*   Customer records in a public utility in the United States.

*Objectives*   A public utility decided to computerise the keeping of customer records. The restructuring of the work performed by twenty-two clerks and six supervisors in the office of a public utility followed this decision to computerise.

*Changes*  The major factor in enriching the unit clerk's routine was bedded in the conscious decision made when computerising to reverse the flow of work between supervisors and clerks. Instead of being distributed by the supervisors to the clerks, work was routed directly to the clerks from the post-room or switch-board and only referred to supervision when the clerk wished to query a more difficult item. The clerks required considerable training for this new task and during a six-month period they gained experience of letter writing, of handling telephone queries, and of the preparation of computer data, all of which were aspects of the 'enriched job'. The clerk was then the public utility's link with 7–8000 consumers and handled about 12,000 measured 'outputs' in a year. Each clerk received about 50 letters per week, half of which needed a reply. Each clerk received or initiated about 20 telephone calls a day and would give and receive back approximately 7 worker's job sheets each week.

The supervisors also had to be trained. Their role changed, more emphasis being placed on performing supervisory duties and spending less time on routine activities associated with the work. During the changeover, supervisors had to watch clerks struggle through particular tasks which they could have performed themselves much more quickly. At this stage, the supervisor was to interfere only when requested to do so by a clerk or if it was very apparent that the clerk was in considerable difficulty.

The group of clerks consistently performed above the measured standards for two years during monitoring. Labour turnover for the section held constant at about 8 per cent despite the composition of the workforce. This consisted predominantly of young married girls between the ages of 20 and 30, who normally only had a short tenure, leaving the job for a variety of domestic reasons.

*Particular problems and issues*  The next step in the development was considered to be the creation of 'natural work units'. These were to bring together a group of clerks to perform a number of associated tasks. However, difficulties were envisaged when attempting to create such schemes. It was not seen to be the reluctance of the clerical staff which hindered such developments but rather the management problems arising from the creation of multifunctional jobs. For instance, it would be likely that a clerk would be cutting across secretarial, accounting, engineering and marketing departments. The managers of each of these were likely to be concerned because of a loss of direct control over the work being done in their department.

It also appeared that reduction in the level of supervision would be possible. Supervisors may well have resented the perceived diminution of their responsibilities and status. Also a reduction in the number of supervisors with the consequent squeeze on promotion prospects might well have had detrimental effects on staff morale and ambition.

Both job enlargement and job enrichment focus attention upon improving the motivational content of individual jobs. Whilst the worker in the enriched job may have much greater freedom, variety and responsibility, little attention is paid in the job redesign to the role of the work group in satisfying both personal and organisation needs. In this and the following section, case examples are considered in which changes that focus on the task of the total work group rather than the jobs of each individual have been implemented. Changes made in this first group of cases led to a reorganisation of the work carried out by the group without any major shift in the authority and responsibility of individual group members.

Changes similar to those reported as part of a job enrichment programme have also been introduced in these cases but the essential difference is that they were introduced on a team rather than an individual job basis. Team members, in some instances, were given direct contact with customers and were required to draft letters. Such teams have often been given responsibility for a specific group of customers based on geographical area, nature of work or alphabetical subdivision. In several cases sections were reorganised on a process rather than a functional basis, i.e. teams have been formed to deal with the complete set of activities to meet customer requirements rather than to handle a specialist part of the process. The outcome of this type of reorganisation has been to make the team responsible for a 'complete task'. In some cases this led to more rapid performance feedback, e.g. in one case clerks who edited and transcribed from income tax returns would not get feedback from verifiers for perhaps three months. By forming working units which brought together editors and verifiers such delays were almost eliminated.

Whilst it is not essential that each employee within the team be able to perform all tasks, it appeared to be advantageous. Greater labour flexibility could lead to reductions in manning and eliminate the need for cover during absence. Multiskilled team members were able to increase work variety by rotation between different tasks. Further interest and increased understanding resulted when the group held weekly meetings to discuss problems and produce ideas for improving the jobs.

## AN EXAMPLE OF TEAM WORKING

*Organisation*   Clerical work in an Irish Bank.

*Objectives*   The ledger department was situated on the first floor of the office building and the only contact that the staff of this department had with customers was through the ledger department representative on the ground floor. The department was responsible for issuing cheque books, balancing accounts quarterly, issuing statements on request, answering and investigating queries re accounts, and showing the books (with daily overdrawn accounts) to the management. Lack of space made it necessary to site the ledger department on the first floor. The siting of this department on the first floor had given rise to additional work. For instance, requests for statements were made by internal telephone from the counterhand to the head ledger clerk who in turn had to ask the statement clerk, who then would obtain the statement and send it by lift to the ground floor. It is interesting to note that the particular physical layout of the work situation led to the necessity for three people to be involved in carrying out this simple task. A similar sequence of steps was necessary in meeting any requirement of management or other staff, e.g. requests for ledger cards, certificates of interest, etc. Many employees found the system frustrating.

*Changes*   The organisation of the ledger department prior to the change could be represented diagrammtically as in Exhibit 8.

A considerable degree of frustration was being experienced by those working in the ledger department, apparently as a result of the routine nature of the work and its fragmentation. It was difficult for an individual to see how the particular piece of work he/she did contributed to the overall effectiveness of the branch or indeed the overall effectiveness of the ledger department. This frustration was further aggravated by the fact that on most days the work did not balance so that on most, overtime had to be worked. In turn this induced a sense of apathy because there seemed to be no way out of the difficulty.

The filing of cheques was divided between four junior clerks from outside the ledger department together with the statements clerk. The division of responsibility for this task and its inherently boring nature led to its not being done regularly and then to the frequent necessity of bringing a larger team back

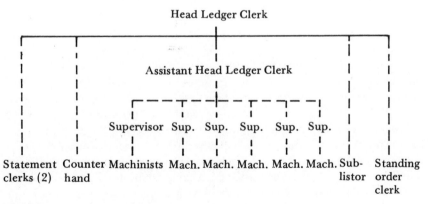

**EXHIBIT 8**   Ledger department organisation

35

on overtime in order to get the filing up to date. Even then the filing was haphazard at best and further problems arose as a result. For instance, the ledger supervisors or statements clerks found it difficult to locate cheques which were being sought and statements often went out to clients with wrong cheques or with cheques missing. With regard to sending out paid cheques together with statements, because of the staff shortage, the practice had been mainly to send out only those which had been specifically requested. This in turn led to overloading of files and consequently made filing even less attractive. Some easing of the situation resulted when a second girl was assigned to this work just before the job redesign project was begun.

Turning to the problem of the daily balancing of the ledger book, over the previous two years new entrants had been put on waste (batch) machines and up to 30 per cent of the errors discovered when balancing the day's work in the ledger department could be attributed to errors made by those operating the waste machines. If the error was made in the waste department or clearing department it still meant that to confirm this all the work had to be checked off, and this had to be done even though the ledger department personnel did their work correctly on that particular day.

The sub-listing work (the listing of large numbers of cheques for individual accounts so that the ledger machinist only had to post a total to the relevant ledger cards) was done by one person who also posted the ledgers and statements of a major client.

In brief, then, the 'pre-change' system was such that most of the staff in the ledger department worked individually; few felt much responsibility for tasks that would contribute to the overall smooth functioning of the ledger department. There was a fairly widespread feeling of 'that's not my job' and little team work existed.

We shall now describe the changes made to the organisation of the ledger department. Broadly speaking the staff of the ledger room were divided into six sections or teams. The new organisation is shown in Exhibit 9. The philosophy being applied was that of creating the atmosphere and qualities of a small office within a large office.

Each team was made responsible for most of the work relating to a particular ledger, i.e. posting, sorting, checking, heading up, showing books, initialling overdrafts up to certain limits, filing cheques, calling ledgers, sending out statements, and answering telephone queries. Initially they did not deal with correspondence, either incoming or outgoing. One team only had two members. Even so, in order to introduce the change one extra member of staff was added to the ledger room. This would have been unnecessary if the standing orders had been split up amongst the six sections but it was thought that such a change was not desirable during the initial stages since, if the change did not work out satisfactorily, it would have been a major task to centralise the standing orders. Certain other tasks which could not be distributed among the teams were assigned as the permanent responsibility of particular teams. For instance, one team got the responsibility for completing the control sheets,

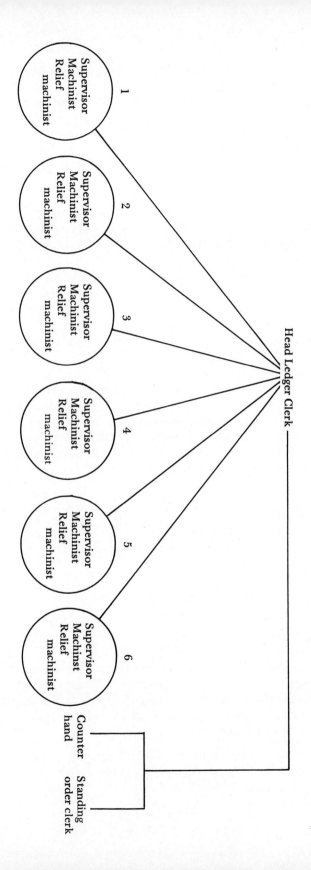

**EXHIBIT 9** Revised ledger department organisation

another had the task of putting away cheques and lodgements and making sure cheques and lodgements were processed by the waste department, and so on.

It was also decided to have the counterhand request as many customers as possible to accept their statements by post. In this way the number of telephone calls to the ledger department was reduced and thus the staff there were able to send out most of the statements to the customer more speedily.

With regard to the showing of the books, instead of supervisors going through the ledgers and entering the overdrawn accounts in the books the ledger clerks took on this task. They gave the completed books to the supervisors who checked off the various accounts and initialled those within their range of discretion. The degree of discretion which supervisors would be allowed had to be decided by management and levels such as £50 to £100, or 5 to 10 per cent in excess of overdraft limits set by management were considered. It was the regular practice for a member of management to go to the ledger room and query teams about accounts which had been initialled. In order to be able to answer such queries satisfactorily at least some team members had to be familiar with sanction and interview books and files. The outcome of this is that a greater knowledge and understanding of accounts is built up amongst the staff.

*Particular problems and issues*

1 The changes resulted in a considerable reduction in the amount of overtime worked. For example, before the change, during the month of October, 618 overtime hours were worked; in November, 397 hours were worked and for December the figure was 552 hours. For the period 10 January (when the new system of working was introduced) to 25 February overtime of the order of 200 hours was worked by the ledger department staff.

2 All staff who were affected immediately by the change regarded the new way of working as more satisfactory than the old system of working.

3 The management of the bank took the view that the staff were more contented than they were before the change.

4 Staff became familiar with a wider range of work.

5 An outside observer was impressed that more teamwork and co-operation existed in the department.

6 Management felt that there may be some waning of enthusiasm for the change as those involved became more accustomed to the change. They also felt that three supervisors had benefited considerably more from the changes than the others. It seemed that for those with a high degree of frustration with their careers and their advancement, changes of a reasonably marginal nature such as those which were typically made in job redesign projects did not lead to increased work involvement.

7 Accounts balanced much more frequently, there was a marked improvement in the filing of cheques, most statements being issued had correct

paid cheques with them, 'heading up' (checking details of ledger cards forward to new ledger cards) which had been customarily checked on overtime was being completed early every morning and, if necessary, being brought up to date in the afternoon. In connection with balancing it is worth noting that with the introduction of the other changes the clerks operating waste machines were required to machine the current account items a second time to ensure that the items negotiated through the office each day were balanced before going to the ledgers. In addition, a more senior official was made responsible for the waste section.

## 4   Semi-autonomous work groups (9 cases)

In these cases either existing or newly created work groups were made responsible for activities more normally under the control of a supervisor or manager. The work group could exercise a greater degree of control over its own work. Often the group was responsible for planning and evaluating its own work in addition to performing tasks. These changes created opportunities for employees to perform 'enriched' work as well as develop skills and experience which prepared them for more responsible work and management jobs.

Supervisors were eliminated from the management hierarchy in several cases. Work groups were given access to technical and other advice, often from former supervisors performing a different role within a support group. In one case in an insurance company the self-managing groups elected their own representative to handle communication flow between management and work group as well as co-ordinating the work of group members. The supervisors in another case became group leaders and were expected to focus more effort upon providing performance feedback to the group than that previously made available.

Work group members, as indicated earlier, were made responsible for a greater degree of planning. Examples of these planning activities included arranging the work rota, scheduling the work, deciding work patterns and the timing of breaks. In many instances the work group activity was designed to include the total process. Training was provided so as to ensure multiskills within the group, work rotation then being practical. Direct customer contact was built into the activities of several groups. For example, increases in the authority assigned to a group of airline booking clerks enabled them to resolve customers' queries without recourse to supervision. The establishment of work standards for this group also created opportunities for self-monitoring. In this case, these changes contributed to a large improvement in efficiency. The work group in several instances became involved in the decisions about changes in the technology and other facilities as well as

39

the actual membership of the work group. *Ad hoc* decision groups in one example, in an insurance company, included representatives of the work group and made decisions concerning transfer of personnel, recruitment, manpower planning and allocation of offices. Regular work group meetings were a feature of several cases. Such discussions were considered essential for agreeing a course of action on many of the issues for which the work group had been made responsible.

In one case annual salary increases were decided within the work group. When all members were in agreement about opening such discussions they met with their section head and another manager to negotiate increases in group salary and its distribution amongst members. Where total agreement was not achieved the group discussed the total salary increase for the group and management decided the allocation amongst members. In another report, disciplining of work group members by colleagues within the group was thought to be more stringent than normal management practice.

## AN EXAMPLE OF A SEMI-AUTONOMOUS WORK GROUP

*Organisation*   Clerical work in a Scandinavian insurance company.

*Objective*   The need to update risk statistics and improve that section's performance.

*Method*   A project group was created to analyse the existing situation, generate alternative solutions and make recommendations to management. This group comprised a department manager as project leader, five other management representatives and six elected employee representatives. A reference group consisting of the section manager, an administration manager, the personnel manager and two training specialists were available to provide all the necessary support services.

The project group members participated in a specially designed one-week course dealing with organisational theory and training in interpersonal skills. Following this, during a five-month study, this group carried out an attitude survey. As a result of their investigation they recommended a series of changes to be made as part of an ongoing development programme. Implementation of changes to the organisation were overseen by a project group including elected employee representatives.

*Changes*   Four central functions (technical, insurance, claims and administration) were established with a management group in each. Each central function was split into work groups without supervisors. Each group was involved in preparing risk statistics, tariff-setting and risk evaluation, duties previously carried out within different sections. A specialist resource group was made available to advise the members of the working group as requested.

Work groups were assigned specific regions within the Eastern zone and carried out all the required tasks for their own customers — previously this would have been processed through several functional work groups. Work groups were differentiated to some extent by the type and size of their customers. They varied in size from five to eight members.

*Outcome*   The changes were introduced nine months after the project group made its recommendations.

*Particular problems and issues*   During the planning stage the initial project group did not succeed in overcoming the problem of providing adequate information on their discussions to the other 200 staff in the section. Written summaries of meetings were not distributed by employee representatives who relied instead on verbal feedback. Many employees had a long service record within the company and whilst very experienced within restricted work areas had only limited knowledge of other activities. They were required to cope with three major changes, i.e. learning new jobs, adapting to new work colleagues and working without a designated supervisor. Training courses were organised during the three months before implementation. Additionally, one-day meetings were organised by the training specialists for each work group covering topics including:

a   How to co-operate in a group.
b   Group norms and common decisions.
c   How to discuss problems together.
d   Likely future problems for the group.

Due to the backlog of work in the risk statistics section, the section was under intense pressure to update these data. In addition to employees working overtime, other resources within the zone were utilised. This delayed development of the skills necessary for the new work organisation. The changes also created much uncertainty. Staff were encouraged to compile lists of both anticipated and actual problems for presentation to management.

## The implementation of change

Many case descriptions concerned with job enlargement, job enrichment, team working and semi-autonomous work groups focused upon the outcomes of change rather than the means by which changes were introduced. However, in this section we will summarise the approaches used to design and implement change.

In many cases consultants were involved in assisting the management of change. In eleven of the cases reported consultants external to the organisation were used; in seven cases consultants internal to the organisation were involved. Either in addition, or as an alternative, in many cases specialists were involved, i.e. personnel department, training, organisation development and O&M.

Groups specifically created for planning change were reported in ten cases. Four of these groups comprised managers exclusively. In the other six, employees or their representatives were engaged along with managers in the planning process. There were no instances in which staff themselves appear to have initiated changes directly, nor any in which the strategy adopted for introducing change was other than the decision of management. The approach and the procedures used seem to reflect the preferred method of the consultant involved. Clearly the consultant may have been selected because he advocated a particular approach.

We have included two case descriptions which illustrate options available to those having to decide an approach to planning change. The first case reflects the approach advocated by a group of American management consultants and is highly structured in that it defines specific stages in the process. These consultants specify that it is the responsibility of management to plan and implement change. The second case involves a British organisation and internal consultants who took a much different approach to planning change. They saw their role as being to assist management and staff jointly in defining problems and working towards a joint solution. They sought to create a new environment in which joint problem-solving would be an ongoing process and that changes introduced at the early stages would not be seen as a final solution but part of a process of development.

## A CASE ILLUSTRATING A STRUCTURED APPROACH TO PLANNING CHANGE

*Organisation*   The data preparation department of a UK manufacturing and distribution organisation.

*Objectives*   To improve morale and reduce labour turnover and absenteeism.

*Project*   The company was a privately owned manufacturer of confectionery items. The office involved in this project was situated in the South East of England. The department had existed for five years when the project commenced. The office was located remote from other Head Office functions.

The department's function was to process orders from fifteen depots totalling between 22,000 and 32,000 orders per month. The order level was influenced by seasonal variations in sales. For the data preparation VDU group this meant an average of about one million key depressions per day. Work was required to be completed by the end of each day. The work required a staff complement of twenty-seven people plus a senior and junior supervisor who reported to the data preparation manager. There was also a computer services manager in the department. Traditionally, the work was separated into four different functions or tasks:

*a*   Part-time clerks recording receipts of orders from the depots into data preparation.

*b*   The punching of the orders.

*c*   Verification to see that the punching is correct

*d*   Transferring the data onto tape and taking tapes to the computer room.

As a result the work of the department was divided into specific tasks which operators were expected to complete.

The data preparation manager initiated the project. He sought the assistance of the personnel department to assess the possibility of a 'job enrichment project' being introduced into data preparation as a means of improving morale, which at the time he felt to be extremely low.

The following steps were taken:

1   After being shown a film and time spent in discussion, the departmental managers were asked to commit themselves to a job enrichment programme.

2   A questionnaire was administered to the staff by the personnel department. This received a 100 per cent response. The responses revealed that:

    *a*   There was general satisfaction with 'hygiene' factors, such as the layout and work environment.

    *b*   The relationships between various groups was a source of dissatisfaction.

    *c*   Achievement feedback and responsibility were seen as low and people perceived themselves as being 'cogs in a wheel'.

The results of the survey were given directly to the staff. Following discussion the problems were then summarised as:

    *a*   Isolation from production and the organisation in general.

    *b*   Staff experiencing feelings of an unfair distribution of the work-load amongst themselves.

    *c*   A lack of information given directly to staff about daily achievements.

    *d*   Concern about the means used for dealing with errors which emanated from the depots and the lack of responsibility at the depots for correcting them.

3   A working party was set up consisting of the two managers, the supervisor and a person from data control (in another department). Following training the working party held six meetings but these were not very productive. The 'key' manager was not always present and the group seemed reluctant to make decisions.

4   Simultaneously weekly meetings were held directly with the employees and this led to certain changes, particularly in 'hygiene' factors such as new decorations and a radio.

5   The working party eventually decided to reorganise the department. Three groups were set up with specific responsibility for certain depots. An analysis of errors was to be carried out in order to improve the feedback to

the depots. A monthly report was to be prepared which analysed each depot's errors. Each team was made responsible for all tasks associated with their allocated depots. Implementation was to be in stages, one team being set up for a six-month trial. This was found to work well; both absenteeism and labour turnover were reduced. After two months, the supervisor requested implementation elsewhere and after three months the other staff themselves requested changes. The other groups were set up in what is traditionally the busiest period of the year. During the first week, following the change, operations were chaotic. However, the supervisor was highly committed to the change programme and discussions were held with each team. In this way problems were discussed and resolved. During the next three months many problems emerged, but the department continued with the scheme. As a result there were considerable improvements in the quality of work and informal 'job and finish' became the accepted practice. The evening shift was no longer necessary since, following the initial period after the change, the staff completed the total work-load in less than a full day.

Factors that appear to have led to the success of the change include:

1    When the changes created 'chaos', the girls were challenged as a group and facts put to them. They then set out to prove that the system was workable.
2    Involvement in target setting led to team members knowing exactly what was required.
3    Organisation into teams led to members making sure that each did her fair share. The teams did not want to admit that an evening shift was necessary.


## A CASE ILLUSTRATING PARTICIPATIVE PROBLEM-SOLVING

*Organisation*   Clerical work in local offices of a Department in the UK Civil Service.

*Objectives*   The two specific objectives for the project were to improve the service given to the customers and to improve the job satisfaction of the staff involved.

*Project*   The major impetus to develop new ways of working in the particular UK Civil Service Department came in 1973, when morale was seen as being particularly low and there was the first ever Civil Service strike. The Second Permanent Secretary in the Department proposed at this time a 'radical and imaginative re-appraisal' of the job of administering the Social Security system with the long-term aim of building 'a sound and sensitive local administration for the next two decades'. The Department's Job Satisfaction Team was invited to assist in this task and a special seven-member Job Satisfaction Team was created to oversee the project.

It was recognised that part of the failure of earlier projects carried out in tax offices was due to factors peculiar to the Civil Service. The original approach to implementing change was later seen as ill-equipped to tackle the problem. In a Civil Service Department project review it was indicated that 'the divide between policy-makers in Whitehall and executive/operational staff in the provinces; the system of checks and counterbalances which had grown up around the concept of public accountability; and a code-of-instruction mentality arising through the pursuit of equity, which defines jobs in terms of rigid procedures rather than end product', were among the factors that had led to the lack of earlier success. It was then decided to initiate a series of experiments at a local level based on the philosophy that people actually doing the job had a better understanding of the local problems than is the case with central administrators.

*Method*   In order to enable experimentation in a local office, it was necessary to obtain the commitment of both executive management and the staff organisation in order that laid-down codes and procedures could be challenged and changes implemented. The Job Satisfaction Team saw their role as assisting employees develop their own solutions and not that of imposing externally determined answers. Consequently there was no question of establishing an experiment in the office unless the local staff approved also. Criteria were established for the choice of the first office — among them were the disposition of the regional controller and his staff, the group manager responsible for the office, the local office manager, the regional and local staff representatives and, not least, the local staff; the geography of the office; the size of the office; etc. A South Wales local office was selected for the first phase of the project. Three months after starting every member of staff had been individually interviewed and work had begun with staff from small sections to tackle the problems identified within their own work area. Fairly quickly the Job Satisfaction Team was under pressure to achieve results within a short time scale and in order to add momentum to the project it put forward suggestions outlining a different form of organisation. The organisational change proposed would result in management staff being 'advisers' rather than the line managers in their own office. The proposed changes in organisation were accepted and executive officers were given responsibility for day-to-day service to customers. They were to be in charge of 'customer service groups' with senior officers acting as group advisers. The management team then determined what form the advisory groups should take and grouped themselves into technical service, training, personnel and monitoring.

Within six months of the completion of the interviewing, considerable change had been made to organisation and layout. Generally, it was thought that the change from line management role to advisor was too abrupt for most of the management team, particularly as they had no opportunity to learn new skills. However, it was felt that the pilot work had sufficiently demonstrated the potential for improvement by working in this new way and two other regions of the Department were selected to develop further projects.

45

Six months later, a second phase of the programme commenced at two offices in the North East. Two small Job Satisfaction Teams consisting of two people (each with one of the original team), moved into these offices. They were joined by a member of the regional staff who was there to gain experience in the type of work being done. In order to involve the local management at an early stage, an initial period was spent by both teams in explaining to senior support staff what the project activity entailed. In both offices the management team and staff were to identify their own issues and develop their own solutions; no change was to be enforced from outside the office.

As a result of the programme of experimentation several conclusions have been drawn:

a   Staff at all levels have, over a period of months, actively concerned themselves with analysing and improving their work organisation and working methods. Whilst many of the changes implemented were not in themselves unique within the Department, these projects were distinguished because of the wide range of innovatory work undertaken in planning and implementing change by all staff at the office from the manager to the clerical assistant.

b   Changes have been achieved with no detriment to performance or output as measured by Department standard indicators.

c   There is enthusiasm at a local level to proceed with the work independent of the Job Satisfaction Team.

Nevertheless concern was expressed by the Civil Service Unions about their level of influence over the project work. It took two further years for these unions to agree to join a steering committee with the Civil Service Department Job Satisfaction Team so as to monitor developments.

Following these initial projects the emphasis changed, in an attempt to broaden the debate, from experimentation to one of consideration of management of offices throughout the Department. Consideration later focused particularly on management style.

## Particular problems and issues in implementing change

The factors most frequently reported as particularly problematic relate to resistance to change. Supervisory resistance to loss of status and power was highlighted in several of the cases as a hindrance in the development of changes to job and work organisation. A change in supervisory attitudes and styles of management was also reported as lacking in one example. Where no change in the organisational climate was detected by the employees, changes in the nature of the tasks performed seemed not to lead to improved morale.

In one instance the supervisors were reported as having reverted willingly to former practices and supervisory style as soon as an opportunity arose. The introduction of increased work group autonomy could possibly lead to a reduction in overall supervisory numbers, a factor which could limit staff development at lower levels. More efficient utilisation of resources could also create clerical redundancies. In some examples staff were redeployed, a policy which may have been acceptable to senior trade union representatives but less acceptable to those directly affected. This may have slowed down the rate of progress where no alternative jobs existed and little natural wastage occurred. Union scepticism about the benefits of job redesign for clerical employees was reported in several instances.

The actual job changes were felt to be superficial and insignificant by employees in one case. In another case staff who were previously disenchanted with their work were reported as less likely to feel greater involvement resulting from job redesign than those who expressed more positive views initially. The impact of the changes in this particular example was felt by management not to be long lasting. Staff soon became accustomed to their new roles.

In one example it appeared that the changes introduced were inappropriate at the point in time. The point was made that morale was particularly low and emphasis was placed upon the redesigning of jobs when other aspects of the motivational package were perhaps of greater priority to staff.

Existing structures, procedures and reward systems may have also restricted opportunities for job redesign. In one case, in a government department, existing grading structures and manpower establishment reduced flexibility for a change at a local level. Also entry requirements demanding 'over-qualified' personnel may have contributed to a mismatch between people and jobs. The need for changes in payment levels to support job redesign seemed to be problematic in larger organisations and became an excuse for not extending projects. The establishment of multiskilled groups of clerks was resisted in one case where each team of clerks would have had to service several departments — the local managers wished to retain control.

The stage at which employees affected by job redesign should be involved in the process was questioned in an example in Belgium. American approaches based on ideas of job enrichment were thought to be not totally suitable in the Belgian culture. Early schemes, as in America, were devised and implemented by management and subsequently changes in the approach were made in order to involve staff directly at a much earlier stage.

Wider diffusion of the ideas was specifically mentioned in one case. Changes were made initially in one section of a bank. The decision regarding implementation of similar changes elsewhere, however, was not being imposed on local management. Where an interest was expressed, support facilities would be made available from a central service department.

## Conclusions

Our survey suggests that a principal goal in many clerical job redesign projects is improvement in efficiency. Thus in many cases there was a trend away from task specialisation as a means of improving overall efficiency. Often over-rationalisation of clerical procedures and processes appeared to have resulted in jobs that were repetitive, disjointed, lacking in responsibility and offering little scope for personal development. The costs associated with such trends in many cases were high labour turnover, absenteeism and difficulty in recruitment. These factors in turn led to inefficiencies in operations through time lost recruiting and training, mistakes, over-manning to cover for absenteeism, etc.

One focus of all the surveyed cases was improvement of the content of jobs to better meet the needs of employees. Attention was paid to attributes of jobs such as variety, responsibility, problem-solving, control over a complete task and direct contact with customers. In many instances the changes focused on the level of the work unit. The work group became involved in planning and evaluating their own work which usually included all the required tasks to complete the process. Often duties more traditionally the responsibility of a supervisor were assigned to the work group. Changes of this type, work organisation changes, in some cases led to, or were initiated, as part of a more major re-organisation of the management structure.

Increasing the opportunities to learn and use new skills was an important part of many of the examples. Clerical work in many organisations was no longer the first stage on a promotional ladder. It was often considered as suitable work for young women and it was assumed that they would only be interested in an occupation to fill the short period between school-leaving and marriage. Companies introducing changes have not adopted this view and have been concerned about the development of these employees through increased involvement and training so that they make a more effective contribution to the organisation as well as enjoying a more satisfying career.

Such changes have not been introduced without difficulties. Change, whilst creating opportunities for some employees, will be perceived by others as a threat to their status and position. The group most threatened was the supervisory level. Instances were reported where the supervisor was required to either become a technical expert and resource to the group, a group leader, or was eliminated totally. The changed role demanded a change in managerial style. Supervisors more generally may not be willing to accept, or may be unable to cope with, the changes demanded. Clearly considerable preparation and support is necessary if supervisors are to be accommodated effectively in the new-style organisations being created.

Detailed planning is required for the implementation of change to be successful. Thorough diagnosis is necessary and decisions have to be made about the appropriateness of job redesign and work organisation change as a means of solving the organisation's problems. The act of planning change raised expectations which may not be met if the resulting changes are minor. Also this planning must include a review of other factors which may limit both the possibilities for job redesign and work organisation change and its long-term impact, e.g. payment structures and information systems, and means must be devised to facilitate changes that are seen as meaningful by employees. Involvement at the planning stage of the employees to be affected by change often leads to more relevant and acceptable changes. The impact of changes upon other sections and parts of the total system must receive careful consideration. Where it is desired that change should spread beyond an initial exercise, a strategy for diffusion must be developed at an early stage. Involvement of employees in every stage of change planning should lead to a smoother implementation of change both in a small-scale exercise and in the wider diffusion throughout the organisation.

The case examples reviewed lead us to suggest that in many companies improvements could be made to clerical jobs which would lead to gains for employees and employer. Additionally, where companies are introducing technological change they should give considerable attention to the design of jobs and work organisation in order to achieve high utilisation of equipment. If the new situation fails to meet the needs of employees the costs associated with high labour turnover, absenteeism and low motivation will require remedial measures which will be expensive in financial and human terms. Opportunities are created through participative planning of job redesign to increase the level of employee involvement and participation in the daily activity of the enterprise at a rate which is appropriate for the employees concerned. Whilst difficulties in planning and executing such changes exist the potential benefits appear to outweigh the costs.

---

**SUMMARY POINTS**

1   Changes in job design and work organisation were aimed at improving both operational efficiency and employee satisfaction.

2   The changes can be categorised as job enlargement, job enrichment, team working and semi-autonomous work groups.

3  Benefits for management and staff were reported from projects where job and work organisation changes were introduced.

4  Two approaches to planning change were identified. The first involved a management working party and a structured approach with defined stages. The second involved a joint management–staff working party and a problem-solving approach.

5  Management and supervisory resistance, existing procedures, reward and grading systems, and the timing of the project were all factors limiting the success of change programmes.

CHAPTER 4

# Principles of job design and work organisation

In the previous chapters we have seen something of the technology available for automating many of the activities undertaken within the office. It is generally recognised that capital investment at the workplace per employee in the average office is well below that in manufacturing. During the next decade, however, this situation is likely to change rapidly. Whilst new technologies have the potential for improving productivity in the office, it has also been indicated that without early consideration of the motivation and reponse of managers and staff to be affected, both directly and indirectly, successful implementation of the changes may not be achieved.

When considering investment in new equipment, the estimated cost of both the hardware itself and the software needed to operate the equipment is invariably considered. Much less emphasis is placed upon the costs involved in retraining, redeployment and redundancy. It seems equally the case that only limited consideration is given to the human aspects of implementation — an area that we believe to be the key to successful implementation.

In this chapter we start by considering what motivates people. We will then consider guidelines that will enable us to design work systems more effectively.

## Motivation — ideas and theories

Our starting point in a consideration of what motivates people is deciding what we mean by the term *motivation*. Often satisfaction and motivation seem to be used synonymously. However, managers generally are more concerned to see that their staff are motivated to carry out the duties assigned than they are that staff should feel satisfied. We believe that in the ideal situation staff are both satisfied and motivated and, further that this ideal is achievable. Neverthless, it is not unusual for people to be dissatisfied with their current job but still be highly motivated to perform well, possibly spurred on by the prospect of promotion. Performance, however, results from the possession of skills and the opportunity for application as well as positive motivation.

Whilst there is no one definition there is general agreement that *motivation* is primarily concerned with:

a    The forces that stimulate human behaviour.
b    The factors that direct or channel such behaviour.
c    The means by which this behaviour is maintained or sustained.

The development of theories of motivation has been influenced by two primary schools of thought. On the one hand supporters of Freud assume that humans are driven by inherited, conflicting, unconscious drives which lead them to behave instinctively. The second group believe that man is a rational being, aware of goals and directing actions so as to achieve these goals. If humans are believed rational in seeking goal achievement, self-control is possible. If, on the other hand, humans are governed by subconscious drives then they probably need direction and control. A simple model of the basic motivation process based on the theory of goal-directed behaviour is illustrated in Exhibit 10. Whilst an oversimplification of an obviously complex process, it serves as a useful starting point.

The view of motivation represented in Exhibit 10 suggests, initially, that there are energetic forces within people that drive them to behave in certain ways in response to external forces. Secondly, there is the idea of an aim or goal to be achieved. Thirdly it suggests that the person learns from experience and an internal feedback mechanism operates. The feedback received will affect the person's future decisions.

People possess desires, needs and expectations such as high status, additional earnings, identification with a group. Where needs are not met the person will experience a sense of disequilibrium and if opportunities are perceived for fulfilling these needs people are likely to take action.

In deciding to take action the person to some extent will weigh up the likelihood of achievement, the cost of failure and the affect upon other people. The response being achieved will lead the person to constantly assess the situation, adjusting actions where thought appropriate.

As pointed out earlier this model is clearly a simplification of an extremely complex process. Difficulties are immediately apparent when one attempts to explain the actions of others. First, motives can be inferred. When observing other people we can infer motives, e.g. he must enjoy gardening because he spends so much time on his own in the garden. Even questioning will often not reveal the 'real truth', either because people hide inner feelings or perhaps are not themselves aware of them. Secondly, there are many needs, desires and expectations

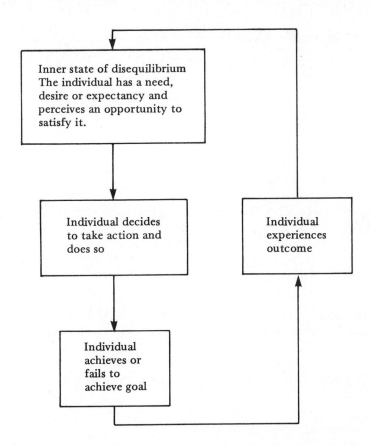

**EXHIBIT 10** A simple model of the basic motivation process based on a model proposed by Dunnette, M.D., and Kirchner, W.K., in *Psychology Applied to Industry,* Appleton-Century-Crofts, New York (1965).

present at any one time and they are given varying priority by individuals at different times. People often have to reconcile different and conflicting needs. Thirdly, the fulfillment of a particular need will not automatically eliminate that need, it may spur a person on to concentrate more effort in that direction, e.g. the athlete who is not satisfied with having achieved a world record, the employee who gains promotion may see himself as having a greater prospect than he previously recognised and as a result strive for further promotion. Finally, we need to consider the differences between individuals in the strength of various needs, their views of how to satisfy these needs and their response to the situation in which they find themselves.

Having considered a general model of the motivation process and noticed some of its limitations we will now go on to consider four theories that have attracted considerable attention. This enables us to consider their relevance to the way we organise work.

# 1 Need hierarchy theory

As early as 1943 Maslow suggested that man's needs can be organised into a hierarchy. He identified the following:

a   *Physiological*   The most basic needs are food and water. When unfulfilled they will be of paramount importance to the individual.
b   *Safety needs*   These include both the protection of self from danger and a secure future.
c   *Love needs*   These are the need for love, affection and belonging. They include both giving and receiving companionship and affection.
d   *Esteem needs*   Individuals have a desire for a stable, firmly based, high evaluation of themselves, for self-respect and for the esteem of others. Feelings of capability and achievement and appreciation of 'worth' lead to feelings of self-confidence, usefulness and adequacy.
e   *Self-actualisation need*   The desire for self-fulfilment, the development of the person to the limit of capability.

As lower-order needs are satisfied, higher needs are believed to become dominant. Whilst there is little research evidence to support Maslow's theory it does have a certain appeal. For the manager it suggests that once basic needs have been met it is necessary to create a climate enabling self-fulfilment if employees are to be motivated further.


# 2 Motivating — hygiene theory

This theory was first proposed by Herzberg in the late 1950s. He suggested that the factors involved in motivating people and leading to job satisfaction are separate from the factors leading to job dissatisfaction. The opposite to a feeling of job satisfaction being a feeling of *no* satisfaction rather than job dissatisfaction and *vice versa.* The factors contributing to job dissatisfaction include company policy and administration, supervision, interpersonal relationships, working conditions, salary, status and security and are referred to as *hygiene* factors. The factors leading to job satisfaction, or *motivators,* are intrinsic to the job and include achievement, recognition for achievement, the work itself, responsibility and growth.

For managers wishing to create positive motivation in employees, Herzberg's theory would indicate the need to create jobs that have motivators present. Where employees are dissatisfied, however, emphasis would be placed upon improving the hygiene factors first. Whilst this theory also has appeal there is considerable controversy about its validity. The principles, however, have been applied in designing jobs and the results achieved have shown promise in many cases.

# 3 Equity theory

Equity theory is based on the idea that a major influence over job performance and satisfaction is the degree of equity, or inequity, that an employee perceives in a work situation. The degree of equity referred to is the ratio of an individual's inputs, such as effort, to outcomes, such as pay, when compared to the same ratio for other comparable groups of employees. Satisfaction is believed to result when equity is perceived to exist, and dissatisfaction exists when the balance is disturbed. Feelings of either guilt or unfair treatment result from a situation perceived by the employee as inequitable. The employee will take steps to reduce the tensions created by an inequitable situation.

Equity theory has implications particularly in the design of reward systems. The use of 'objective measures' as the basis for determining pay levels can increase the likelihood of equity being perceived.

# 4 Expectancy/valence theory

Positive valence is a person's preference for attaining a particular outcome. An outcome has a zero valence when a person is indifferent to attaining it. Outcomes also can have either a negative or a positive valence. Decision-making, however, involves an element of risk and when choosing a course of action the individual will weigh up both personal preferences (valences) and the likelihood of achievement. The word 'expectancy' is used to define the momentary belief concerning the likelihood that a particular act will be followed by a particular outcome. Motivation, then, is the force resulting from the combination of valence and expectancy.

For positive motivation to be present the values of both valence and expectancy must differ from zero. A person will only be motivated to perform well if such performance has the highest score of 'Expectancy × Valence'. Factors believed to determine a person's level of expectancy include the actual situation and past experience of a similar situation, personality factors (people with low self-esteem tend to underestimate the likelihood of success) and other people's opinions.

Self-esteem, although relatively stable in mature individuals, can be raised by providing the right kind of jobs and leadership. The person's view of the particular situation will be strongly influenced by the reality of the situation. Therefore, leadership behaviour, pay and promotion systems and the job itself can all influence the estimate of particular behaviour leading to particular outcomes.

No one theory in itself is sufficient to explain employee behaviour. Since inadequacies exist in each it is necessary to extract the main features in order to enable useful analysis of motivational problems. It appears that man is far more complex than is suggested by existing theoretical models. Man's motives may vary in different situations and in addition to being complex within himself he is also likely to differ from his neighbour in the patterns of his own complexity. Experiences appear to lead to new patterns of motivation. Hence, the individual's pattern of motivation results from the interaction between initial needs and organisational experiences. Personality traits, skill level, job knowledge, interactions with co-workers and managers, the nature of the task and the organisational setting are some of the factors that interact in complex fashion to determine the individual's level of motivation.

Here we are concentrating on aspects of jobs and work organisation that the manager can and should consider when designing new systems or diagnosing motivational problems in existing systems. Employees have requirements of their work other than those usually covered by a contract of employment (wages, hours, security of employment, etc.). The following list represents at least some of the general psychological requirements sought in relation to the job*:

a   The need for the content of the job to be reasonably demanding in terms other than just physical effort and yet providing some variety.
b   The need to be able to learn on-the-job and develop personally through the job.
c   The need for some area of decision-making that the individual can call his own.
d   The need for support and recognition at the workplace.
e   The need to feel that one's job is acceptable to others outside the workplace.
f   The need to feel that the job leads to some sort of desirable future.

If jobs are to meet these psychological needs, consideration has to be given to their design. It has to be recognised that not all individuals share the same level of psychological need strength and that some workers are satisfied with jobs appearing to others as highly repetitive, low in skill-demand and responsibility. We must, therefore, consider methods for developing flexibility at the workplace so that individuals have some opportunity for personal development.

## Job design, work-group organisation and employee motivation

From this brief overview of motivation theories it is clear that many factors combine to determine the direction and level of employee motivation. Focusing now on one area, i.e. job design and work organisation, certain principles have been identified. Herzberg, following the exposition of his two-factor theory, was influential in initiating experimentation focusing upon manipulating jobs and work

*Based on Emery, F., and Thorsrud, E., *Democracy at work,* Leiden, Martinus Nijhoff, 1976.

organisation. The emphasis in this research was upon developing jobs so that they had potentially greater degrees of those features classified as motivators. Attention was paid to aspects contributing to achievement, growth, responsibility, recognition of achievement and the work itself.

The expectancy theory has also been developed by later researchers who concentrated upon aspects of work such as variety, autonomy, task identity, feedback, dealing with others and friendship opportunities. Those employees who have an interest in self-development have responded positively to job redesign in situations where other factors are not diverting attention. Herzberg suggested that in situations where hygiene factors are inadequately provided for staff, dissatisfaction will often occur. Where hygiene factors are improved the staff may no longer be dissatisfied but will not automatically be satisfied. For job redesign to result in positive employee response, it would appear that these negative aspects must be resolved either before commencement or at the same time as the work itself is tackled.

It would seem that job performance and satisfaction are also influenced by the degree of equity, or inequity, perceived in the work situation. From this theory we can conclude that, where job and work organisation changes are introduced, employee performance and satisfaction is unlikely to increase unless those employees see themselves as equitably rewarded for their additional contribution.

Previous research has led to the identification of attributes contributing to employee motivation that can be used as the basis for the design of jobs. These principles, against which jobs can be assessed, are described in Exhibit 11. We shall now examine each principle in turn.

Variety in the job can result from a range of different features. There may be a wide range of operations in the work or it may be necessary to use a variety of equipment and/or procedures. There may be variety as a result of changes in the product or service and also in the customer receiving that product or service. Variety may be the result of changes in the external environment.

Repetitiveness is distinguished from variety since there may be considerable variety in the task but at the same time the task may be repeated at regular intervals. The more repetitive the task, the more easily learnt. The extent of continuing challenge is likely to be less in highly repetitive work than situations where the task, whilst containing similar features, is capable of being tackled in many different ways.

Some tasks, once mastered, can be carried out without attention. Reflexes become automatic and one can let one's mind wander whilst performing the task. It becomes possible to talk, listen to music, or daydream whilst doing this sort of work. At the other end of the spectrum some jobs are totally absorbing mentally, whilst demanding considerable attention. However, there are many jobs between these extremes which, whilst not mentally absorbing, require sufficient

| 1 | An optimum level of variety |
|---|---|
| 2 | An appropriate degree of repetitiveness |
| 3 | Appropriate degrees of attention with accompanying mental absorption |
| 4 | An optimum level of responsibility for decisions and degree of discretion present |
| 5 | Employee control over his own job |
| 6 | The presence of goals and achievement feedback |
| 7 | Perceived contribution to a socially useful product or service |
| 8 | Opportunities for developing friendships |
| 9 | Where dependent upon others for task achievement some influence over the way the work is carried out |
| 10 | Perceived skill utilisation |

**EXHIBIT 11**   Principles for the design of jobs

attention to make it difficult to talk or concentrate on other activities whilst working.

The level of responsibility and accountability present in the job and the degree to which discretion is permissible in decision-making are important considerations when designing jobs and work organisation. Decision-making can be of a routine nature, governed by previously specified rules, or it can be non-routine in nature and involve the implementation of creative solutions to unstructured problems. The significance of the decisions may be assessed in monetary terms, e.g. the cost of wrong decisions, but normally monetary values cannot be ascribed. Decisions may also be classed as operational, tactical, strategic and policy. Normally the time scale of decisions reflects the significance to the organisation and the level at which such decisions are made in the organisation.

Employee motivation is likely to be affected by the degree to which that employee can control his own job. In many instances machines control the rate of work and monitor employee contribution. Also, work methods are often prescribed by management, sometimes with the assistance of O&M specialists. The extent to which the worker can decide when to do the work, how to do the work and where to do the work will influence that employee's motivation. Additionally, where employees have routine problems to resolve, the extent to which they can resolve them will be important, e.g. resolving problems of poor materials or securing maintenance services.

The presence of definite goals for work output in terms of quality and quantity and achievement feedback are important elements of the job.

Without clearly defined goals the employee is uncertain about the acceptability of his contribution. Yardsticks will then be based possibly upon the performance of colleagues or the individual's previous performance. Unless there is feedback of results and analysis of performance the employee is unlikely to perceive the need to change and less likely to actively seek means by which improvement may be made.

An important aspect of the job is its overall purpose. Employees appear to welcome work that they perceive as clearly contributing to a product or service of value to the community at large. For the individual, recognition and social status is influenced by the rating placed on this contribution by others in society. Task identity is influenced also by the extent to which employees do an entire or whole piece of work and can clearly identify the results of their own efforts.

Many employees value highly opportunities to make social contacts and develop friendships through work. Not only may these opportunities be made available through sports and social activities but the actual design of the job, work organisation and layout can also considerably affect the development of friendships. Noise levels and the positioning of the workplace relative to others will influence the extent to which optional interaction is possible whilst working. Additionally, a job requiring employees to deal with other people (customers or other employees) in order to complete the work will provide opportunities to develop friendships. Jobs also vary in the extent to which employees are free to leave the workplace and the discretion afforded to decide the length of absence.

In many jobs successful achievement of the task involves co-operation between several people. Where such dependency exists, consideration should be given to means by which each individual involved can influence the way the work is carried out.

The last job attribute contained in Exhibit 11 is perceived skill utilisation. The time required to learn to perform the job proficiently is an indicator of the skills demanded. These skills may be manual, involving high degrees of dexterity, precision and manipulation, or mental, involving the application of particular specialist knowledge or skills.

In certain circumstances it may be more appropriate to consider the design of the work group and its activities rather than the design of each individual job. Membership of a work group can have certain positive benefits for the individual. Earlier, we referred to social opportunities at work. When tasks are interdependent membership of the group at least assists in sustaining communication and developing an understanding between team members. Beyond this the work group may develop to a stage where standards of co-operation are enforced and mutual help and support is available. Membership of a work group can also have positive benefits where the work is particularly stressful since support from others experiencing similar problems can help overcome the difficulties. Focus on the group task can also facilitiate the development of a complete and meaningful task where subdivision of the work to individuals would result in a series of fragmented activities.

Exhibit 12 contains principles for the design of the work group and its activities. The emphasis here is upon defining the tasks and responsibilities of the work group. Individuals within the group are then afforded the opportunity to develop with other team members their own role within that group. Objectives for the group are to be clearly established but the means for achieving them are the responsibility of the work group members. The size of the group is an important consideration . If too few tasks are assigned to the group there will not be sufficient flexibility within the range of activities to enable staff to develop a variety of roles. Also, social opportunities will be more restricted. As the group increases in size agreement will be more difficult to attain and fragmentation of the group more likely. Group performance over time can be improved if members are involved in both the planning and evaluation of their own work. This can lead to an increased knowledge of the work and its relevance to the organisation in total as well as increased understanding of how best to organise the work group. Involvement in monitoring performance also gives an opportunity for members to improve problem-solving skills. Additionally it gives individuals the feedback about their contribution which has been frequently referred to as an important element in the motivation process.

Having considered the definition of the task for the group and the involvement of members in planning and evaluation we can turn

| 1 | In the office primary work groups should include between four and ten members |
| 2 | The primary work group should have a designated leader who is accountable for the group's performance |
| 3 | The group should be responsible for activities which make up a complete task |
| 4 | Wherever possible the group members, through their supervisor or manager, should be responsible for planning their own work |
| 5 | Members should have the opportunity to evaluate their performance compared with the standards set for the job |
| 6 | All the skills necessary for satisfactory task achievement must be present within the group or alternatively easily accessible |
| 7 | Reward systems should be designed to support group behaviour |

**EXHIBIT 12**  Principles for the design of work groups

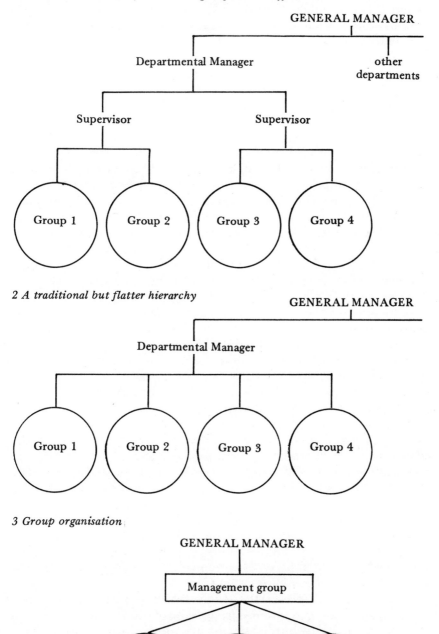

*1 A traditional hierarchy with work groups in the office*

GENERAL MANAGER

Departmental Manager

other
departments

Supervisor

Supervisor

Group 1

Group 2

Group 3

Group 4

*2 A traditional but flatter hierarchy*

GENERAL MANAGER

Departmental Manager

Group 1

Group 2

Group 3

Group 4

*3 Group organisation*

GENERAL MANAGER

Management group

Group 1

Group 2

Group *n*

**EXHIBIT 13**   Alternative means for managing work groups

attention to the group's relationships with the wider organisation. Whilst group members may be able to effectively manage their own internal organisation, the group's activities have to link into the wider organisation and its objectives. Where work is organised on a group basis there is a need for management of both the interface between groups at any level as well as between groups at different levels and the management hierarchy in general. In Chapter 3 we reported different approaches adopted in practice. Some possibilities are illustrated in Exhibit 13. The first organisation shown in this Exhibit is an example of team working similar to the description in Chapter 3. Here the supervisor still has responsibility for the work group and its activities. However, the supervisor is no longer expected to direct each individual within the team but rather to permit a greater degree of work sharing within the team. The supervisor is expected to deal with the team directly rather than with individuals from it. The role is supportive rather than directive, with the supervisor tending to advise and assist rather than instruct.

The second form of organisation in Exhibit 13 represents the semi-autonomous work group. Here the level of supervision has been reduced. The work group has taken on many of the former responsibilities of the supervisor. It is normal practice, however, for the group to designate specific duties to group members in order that those outside the work group who interface with the work group have satisfactory lines of communication. This co-ordinating role may be rotated amongst group members but it is essential that others in the organisation who need such communication are aware of the individual to whom the task has been designated.

In the third form of organisation the first level of management is also shown as organised on group principles. In the illustration the departmental level of management has been formed into an advisory team comprising the different specialists found at this level. Within this team the expertise might include O&M, communications, training, etc., as well as line managers. Again the management role will be primarily advisory. This group will be involved in negotiating the work of the lower-level groups, including outputs and standards, and in negotiating resources and rewards. Further intervention will be minimised and occur either when requests are made for assistance or when a lower-level group clearly has problems in self-organisation.

The guiding principles for the design of work groups can be applied in different forms of organisation. The question of which form to adopt will be influenced by factors such as the form already existing, the acceptability of introducing alternatives, the skills and abilities of management and staff, the nature of the work, the overall cost-effectiveness of each alternative and the future needs of the organisation. It is clear that no one organisational form is appropriate in all situations and it seems likely that 'tailor-made' solutions will be needed for each situation.

## Conclusions

A brief review of theories of motivation in this chapter revealed that no one theory is adequate in itself to explain employee motivation and behaviour. Many factors appear to inter-relate in complex fashion to determine the extent and direction of employee motivation. However, we identified certain psychological requirements of individuals relating to job content. These requirements resulted from a distillation of the theories expounded by psychologists and others rather than from any one theory. We also recognised that individuals vary in the relative emphasis they place upon each of these requirements.

We examined in some detail principles for the design of jobs and work group activity. The principles advanced relate to the psychological requirements discussed. They enable an assessment to be made of existing workplace arrangements as well as an evaluation of alternatives. They can form part of a framework for diagnosing motivational problems at work. Other factors also need consideration when diagnosing motivational problems. Our emphasis here has been upon achieving a match between the personal and social needs of the individual and the overall objectives of the organisation by designing effectively the job and work group activity. Any mismatch, however, might be the result of inappropriate recruitment policies and practices. Equally employee dissatisfaction may result from other factors within the organisation, e.g. perceived low financial reward, supervisory style, organisational climate, interpersonal problems. Whilst recognising the relevance of these other aspects to the level of employee motivation, we have focused attention on the aspects of work normally most readily manipulated by the line manager in an organisation, i.e. jobs and work organisation.

In the next chapter we will report the findings from an action research project. This project was set up in order to give managers the opportunity to better understand employee motivation and resultant action by tackling their own management problems and evaluating progress. Whilst the principles for the design of jobs and work group activity formed the basis of a framework for diagnosis many other interconnected factors were considered.

---

### SUMMARY POINTS

1    Motivation theory seeks to explain what stimulates human

behaviour, what directs or channels that behaviour and finally the means by which it is maintained or sustained.

2   To date, no one theory of motivation, in itself, reliably predicts human behaviour.

3   Principles for the design of individual jobs have been described.

4   The work group and its organisation in many situations is a more appropriate level to consider when designing organisations than each individual job. Benefits can result for both the staff and the employer where the organisation is built around work groups.

5   It is recommended that management structures should also be reviewed.

# CHAPTER 5

# *Tackling work organisation problems*

In previous chapters we considered different approaches to tackling motivational problems in the office and developed principles for the design of jobs and work group organisation. In this chapter we will examine the application of these ideas in overcoming problems faced by operational managers in managing clerical functions.

The action projects reported on in this chapter and described in the case studies were set up with the deliberate intention of assisting those managers participating to identify and tackle problems. The twelve participants were selected because they were either experiencing difficulties or anticipated changes that would severely disrupt working patterns and relationships.

Several workshops were organised over a 14-month period for participating managers as well as meetings with participants in their own organisation. Case material was developed from information collected prior to the first workshop as well as during the twelve months following the initial changes.

The projects described were undertaken in organisations varying considerably in size from a localised distributor with less than 100 employees to a multinational company with many thousands. The situations also varied considerably, including accounts departments, secretarial services, telephone sales, marketing administration, administrative services and reprographics. The staff numbers involved in sections ranged from five to twenty-three. In several cases the section was within a larger department and ideas successfully implemented were later extended to cover larger areas of the operation.

The problems being considered were varied. Many could be seen as the result of inadequate consideration of the impact of change upon people by those responsible for introducing new technology. Others were directly concerned with the question of how best to introduce new technology. The focus in all the projects was upon managers taking action to improve both operational performance and staff satisfaction.

We have summarised some of the main points from the case studies in this chapter. Readers are referred to the case studies themselves for further detail. The material is presented in the sequence of the problem-solving process, i.e. problems being tackled, actions proposed, implementation and results. We have attempted where possible to construct lists. This was done in order to enable managers in a similar position to have a checklist against which to analyse their own situations. Checklists also provide ideas for change. A further advantage of this approach is that it enables cross-referencing to material in the case studies. This enables the reader to make more selective use of the case material.

## Problems being tackled

Data about the nature of the problem facing managers responsible for clerical functions were collected by questionnaire prior to the first workshop, during a presentation by each manager at that workshop and by inference from actions proposed following the workshop. In some instances a specific outcome resulting was indicated and noted. The data are summarised in Exhibit 14.

Many managers felt that problems were being experienced in motivating employees and that these were the result of the lack of variety present in the jobs. This lack of variety was observed as leading to boredom, low job satisfaction, lack of interest, delays and errors. This lack seems also to have been linked to fragmentation of the work. Where jobs were highly subdivided it was less likely that staff would appreciate the overall process and purpose.

In half of the cases the managers were being pressured to reduce staff numbers. Staff morale then appeared low, in part as a result of feelings of uncertainty. Where staff reductions were aimed for, the flexibility of staff in undertaking alternative work appeared particularly important. The ability and willingness of staff to transfer to other work or expand their own job was seen as a key factor influencing success in implementing change. Managers faced with the problem of surplus staff felt that they would have to familiarise themselves with the availability of alternative jobs and opportunities for staff to transfer, and take a positive role in assisting staff in the change.

A lack of opportunities for development and promotion was seen by several managers as resulting in low staff motivation. This was seen as a particular problem where older staff were not suitable for promotion but had mastery of a relatively simple job which then no longer offered them challenge. Opportunities to be involved in problem-solving and to have 'meaningful' responsibilities were also indentified as a positive source of motivation.

| Problem area/issue | Case study number* | | | | | | | | | | | | Particular outcomes |
|---|---|---|---|---|---|---|---|---|---|---|---|---|---|
| | 1 | 2 | 3 | 4 | 5 | 6 | 7 | 8 | 9 | 10 | 11 | 12 | |
| 1 Variety/work | ✓ | ✓ | ✓ | ✓ | ✓ | ✓ | ✓ | | | ✓ | ✓ | ✓ | Boredom, low job satisfaction, lack of interest, delays, errors |
| 2 Fragmented task | | | ✓ | | ✓ | | | | | | | | Unaware of total process |
| 3 Flexibility | | | | | | ✓ | | ✓ | ✓ | | | | Lack of opportunities |
| 4 Skills/understanding | | | | | | | | ✓ | ✓ | | | | Lack of opportunities |
| 5 Opportunities — promotion, etc. | ✓ | | ✓ | | | | | ✓ | ✓ | | | | Particularly for older people |
| 6 Problem-solving opportunities | | | | | ✓ | | | | | | | | |
| 7 Responsibility | | | | ✓ | | | | | | | | | |
| 8 Involvement | ✓ | | | | | | | ✓ | ✓ | | | | |
| 9 Challenge | | | | | | | | | ✓ | | | | Boredom |
| 10 Status | | | | | | | ✓ | | | | | | |
| 11 Comparability | | | ✓ | | ✓ | | | | | | | | |
| 12 Team spirit | | | ✓ | | ✓ | | | | | | ✓ | | Lack of task sharing/helping, task focus |
| 13 Relationships between sub-systems | | | | | | ✓ | | | | | | | Lack of control over workload |
| 14 Supervisory style | | | | | ✓ | | | | | ✓ | | ✓ | Avoidance of responsibility |
| 15 Role uncertainty | | | | | | | | | | ✓ | | ✓ | Anxiety, friction |
| 16 Feedback | | | | | ✓ | | | | | | | | |
| 17 Operational | | | | | | | | | | | ✓ | ✓ | |
| 18 Office layout | | | | | | ✓ | | | | | | ✓ | Efficiency, social contact, control |
| 19 Change | | ✓ | | | | | ✓ | | | | | ✓ | |
| 20 Staff reductions | ✓ | | | | | | | ✓ | ✓ | ✓ | | | Uncertainty, low morale |

* See Case Studies for the detailed reports (pp. 123 et seq.).

**EXHIBIT 14** Problems and issues identified by workshop participants

67

Several managers reported problems regarding job status and reward. Staff in several cases were reported to compare their status and reward unfavourably with other occupational groups. Some staff believed their jobs to be of greater worth than that established by job evaluation exercises.

As indicated in an earlier chapter many tasks required a team effort if they were to be achieved effectively. A lack of willingness to assist colleagues was noted in two cases. Individuals were seen as concentrating upon their particular aspect of the total task and concerned to achieve that without regard to the wider problems of the work group. In one case the team was seen as lacking control over its workload because they were unable to influence the rate of work of other departments. In this case, the problems experienced appeared to result from operational difficulties.

The supervisory style was seen as inappropriate in two cases. In one instance the supervisor was not fulfilling the responsibilities of the role. In another case a lack of delegation was believed to result in a high level of reliance upon supervision and an unwillingness on the part of staff to accept any responsibility. Where staff were uncertain of the boundaries to their own role and responsibilities there appeared to be personal anxiety and friction between staff.

The actual physical layout of the office was believed by two managers to be contributing to the problem of low staff motivation. In one case the office was overcrowded as well as being situated alongside an industrial area. This office and its location was seen by staff as unsuitable. In the other case the position of the manager's office tended to create feelings in one group for which he had responsibility of being constantly watched whilst the other group was not in the manager's field of vision. In another case the manager was having to decide the layout for new offices.

Changes in the nature of office work resulting from the introduction of new technologies were causing managers some concern. In one instance, one question to be resolved was the appropriate division of work. Another was how to implement changes. Implementation was usually to be accompanied by staff reductions. For those still to be employed in the new situation, however, problems were seen of selecting appropriate training methods, and difficulties were anticipated during system change-over, particularly in coping with the pressures created for management and staff. The changes planned included changes in technology and systems. The changes were anticipated to impact as much upon the manager's job as those of his staff. In most cases the managers appeared to have had little influence over decisions about new systems and equipment.

Here we have summarised the problems reported relating to the management of office functions and staff motivation. One objective of the investigation was to assist managers to better understand the nature of problem-solving and change management within their own context. The data reported reflected the manager's insight and ability to diagnose the problems in his own working environment. In no instance at this stage were data available which were collected specifically for the purpose of diagnosing problems, e.g. attitude survey. One of the questions asked during the first workshop related to the methods to be adopted for a more thorough diagnosis. It was assumed that participants would develop an increased understanding of factors influencing practical office management and staff motivation as a result of planning, implementing and evaluating changes in the office.

## Proposed actions

Each participant prepared an action plan during the course of the first workshop. These plans were to include a statement of objectives as well as steps to be taken to achieve the objectives. The objectives stated in some instances were general, e.g. 'to organise jobs in a far better way than at present'. In other cases the objectives were more specific, e.g. 'to ensure new computerised system is designed in such a way that boredom and lack of interest does not produce errors, indifference or restrict initiative'. None of the action plans included a statement of how the outcomes would be evaluated. In some cases action plans dealt with a proportion of the factors seen as contributing to the problem.

Broadly, action plans focused to differing degrees on three areas relating to the change project, i.e.:

1    Data collection, synthesis and decisions to be made.
2    An outline of changes to be implemented.
3    The approach to be adopted for implementing change.

Two managers present were experienced O&M specialists and both produced action plans that included a more detailed study of the problem. Both proposed a review of existing procedures and equipment. In one case feasibility of increased computerisation of clerical procedures was to be examined. Two further action plans included an examination of the total work-load and its allocation.

Several managers specified actual changes to be implemented. One plan for a sales accounting department contained the following six action points to be achieved within six months:

1    Increase variety of each individual clerk's workload by extending functions to include problem-solving related to their tasks.
2    Increase variety by training clerks in operations associated with use of Burroughs minicomputer.
3    Improve understanding of their tasks by arranging visits to outside

69

plants and training sessions with other areas in sales accounting.

4　Carry out measurement of existing work-loads to determine equitability between clerks.

5　Introduce a daily progress report for completion by clerks as a measure of their performance.

6　Produce job descriptions for each member of the section and define group objectives.

In this case, number five in Exhibit 13, the manager had the authority to implement these changes without recourse to superiors.

The objectives set by the manager for a reprographics department (Case 8), were to create an environment in which operators were motivated and to ensure means for career progression. He proposed the following changes, also setting up target dates:

1　Restructure the Grade 10 jobs to become Grade 9 — to be prepared for re-evaluation in nine months.

2　Operate a rota-system between various work activities within the section — to follow item 1.

3　Involve operators in future equipment selection — immediate.

4　When future staff reductions occur, involve operators in administrative duties — possibly two to three years.

5　Develop day-release schemes into clerical service units — at discretion of manager's superior.

The actions proposed were not generally possible without the authority of this manager's superior.

The need to gain the agreement of other parties to change was recognised in most action plans. In one case the commitment of the computer department to provide facilities for an interim system was seen as the key problem. One of the O&M specialists (Case 11) included two actions aimed at gaining commitment, i.e.:

1　Gain commitment from staff on the need for analysis of the work-load and a study of the situation: use volume increase as the motive; develop relationship with superiors.

2　Sell ideas to supervisor and gain agreement on problem areas.

These action points appear to reflect the O&M specialists' approach to investigating problems and influencing change. As a service department making recommendations to operating managers there is perhaps an emphasis on 'selling ideas'.

Several managers in their action plans appeared to have assumed that by involving staff in examining the problem and developing the solution, there would be greater commitment to the changes. Involvement in problem-solving was also seen as a means for helping employees adapt to new forms of work (computerised routines) as well as a means for creating staff interest. In one instance (Case 1) where VDUs were to be introduced and computerised routines were to replace manual procedures in an accounts receivable section, the manager proposed the following with regard to trials of the new system:

1 Consider behavioural implications.
2 Generate ideas about 'best way of working'.
3 Assessment involving management and those who have worked it.

In Case 2, where new computer routines were to be introduced for a final accounts department, the manager proposed to involve staff in the detailed planning for implementation.

Where an objective was to develop openness between management and employees (Case 6), the manager proposed that the situation should be examined by staff meeting together. Staff were also to be involved in devising the new jobs when VDUs were introduced.

In Case 7 the company was already committed to a policy of involving staff in decisions which would affect their jobs. The word-processing system and the creation of administrative service units was to be introduced gradually with two trial units initially. An experimental approach to organising work was proposed with staff carrying out the analysis for four weeks following the settling-down period.

A summary of the proposed actions is presented in Exhibit 15. Actions are related to those problems and issues identified by participants. In many instances the action proposed was seen by participants as likely to reduce the influence of several factors contributing to low morale. It seems likely that the assumption was also made that action directed at alleviating one problem would also reduce a secondary problem. Also the assumption appears to have been made that the change process itself would reduce some problems. This was particularly likely where involvement of all parties in a collaborative change programme was seen to be a means for changing supervisory style. The focus of most of the actions proposed was the individual job. Most were aimed at increasing variety and hence interest. Means for the development of skills and understanding, creating opportunities and increasing staff flexibility also attracted much attention. These factors also appear important when facing change. Staff training predominates as a means for developing and implementating change.

## Implementation and results

Following the first workshop, participants were requested by the authors to complete a diary of major decisions and events having an impact upon actions proposed. The purpose of this diary was to enable a review of the implementation of actions. Reviews were carried out at

| | Problem area/issue | Action proposed |
|---|---|---|
| 1 | Variety/work simplification | Projects aimed at improving efficiency. Involve in assessing new equipment. Re-allocate work. Rotate jobs. Visits to other locations. Involve in problem-solving. Include computer input tasks in jobs. Experiment with alternatives. Share 'chores'. Allocate jobs in a way that maintains variety. |
| 2 | Fragmented task | Visit other locations and train in other accounts functions. Combine customer contact and order preparation to provide a complete job. |
| 3 | Flexibility | Training in other jobs and operation of rotation scheme. |
| 4 | Skills/understanding | Improve understanding of total process by visits to other locations and training in other accounts functions. Training to prepare for changes in technology. Involve staff during changes in order to develop understanding, skills and competence. |
| 5 | Opportunities – promotion, etc. | Training in use of computer terminal and basic programming. Training in jobs outside department on day-release scheme. Assign administrative duties to staff. Involve older employees in training junior staff. |
| 6 | Problem-solving opportunities | Projects aimed at improving efficiency. Increase extent to which staff involved in investigatory work. Group problem-solving. |
| 7 | Responsibility | Make staff checking invoices responsible for resolving problems. Assign administrative duties to staff. |
| 8 | Involvement | Involve in assessing new equipment. Involve in study groups with customer departments. |

| 9 | Challenge | Training to prepare for changes in technology. Involve in study groups with customer departments. |
| 10 | Status | |
| 11 | Comparability | Measure workloads. |
| 12 | Team spirit | Define group objectives. Delegate to and involve the team. |
| 13 | Relationships between sub-systems | Make an employee responsible for liaison with other departments. |
| 14 | Supervisory style | Involve in management/staff problem-solving. |
| 15 | Role uncertainty | Produce job descriptions and define objectives. |
| 16 | Feedback | Daily reporting system. |
| 17 | Operational | Analysis of workload and study of situation. Document clerical system and isolate duplication and short cuts. Consider increased use of computer. Increase training to reduce errors. |
| 18 | Office layout | Group problem-solving. Design to create a friendly atmosphere. |
| 19 | Change | Involve staff in generating ideas about 'best way of working'. Involve staff in assessing new equipment and considering behavioural implications. Involve staff in planning implementation. Training in new systems. Involve staff in progress reviews. Investigate problems encountered by other companies when introducing similar changes. |
| 20 | Staff reductions | Create training opportunities to facilitate transfer. Examine redeployment opportunities. |

**EXHIBIT 15**  Problems and issues and actions proposed

73

approximately six- and twelve-month intervals. The outcomes are summarised in this section.

## Increasing variety at work

Measures aimed specifically at increasing the level of variety present in the job were taken in two cases. In Case 9 additional tasks were assigned to clerical staff. The supervisor expressed the view that younger workers resented being requested to do additional tasks. However, the response may have been influenced both by the manner adopted by the manager in requesting that additional tasks be undertaken and the interest shown by the departmental managers concerned in expanding the clerk's role.

In a reprographic department (Case 8) steps were being taken to involve staff in planning a job rotation scheme. The development of the scheme, however, was dependent upon a re-evaluation of one of the jobs. At the time, this job was a grade lower than the others in the section. The nature of the work in this job and the skills required were significantly different from other jobs in the section, hence rotation offered fairly considerable increases in variety.

A re-allocation of duties was arranged during staff meetings in an accounts department (Case 2). The group identified training needs relating to the implementation of new systems. Their preferred reorganisation of work was not possible without changes to rules about access to confidential data which senior management later approved. During the implementation of changes further problems arose because of staff shortages.

## Increasing responsibility and accountability

Changes aimed at increasing responsibility and accountability in a sales accounting department were introduced in Case 5. Here clerks were required to identify themselves on all correspondence with other parts of the organisation. Queries about accounts were then directed to the clerk responsible. The supervisor was delegated additonal work by the manager and expected to encourage clerks to resolve more of their own queries. Some clerks expressed concern about the new responsibilities and were inclined to seek help from the supervisor. It was thought that experience would lead to greater confidence. Generally, however, clerks welcomed the change in responsibility and the increased contact with remote locations. Clerks in another accounting department had also become more involved in resolving specific queries. Expansion of the job in this case also resulted in staff becoming more flexible and skilled; it created increased staff interest and understanding of the overall task. In the reprographics department (Case 8) delegation of administrative duties to one clerk in the group was seen as having certain problems. A

74

further tier of supervision was not believed desirable and it also diminished the potential role of the assistant supervisor. More fundamental questions about departmental organisation seemed appropriate in this case.

*Project work*

Special investigations had been assigned to clerks in three accounting departments (Cases 1, 2 and 4). In Case 1, projects were introduced to increase job interest. Well devised project work carried out under appropriate supervision was used to assist trainee accountants in developing professional knowledge and expertise. Also, if well executed, projects could have made a significant contribution to departmental efficiency. In this case, those clerks with a career orientation responded positively to the project work. The manager, however, reported difficulties in identifying suitable topics. Also in a department with little slack resource difficulties existed in releasing clerks from other duties. In Case 2 the manager reported that one clerk was reluctant to become involved in a project designed partly for her own development. Special assignments were to be undertaken within sub-groups in Case 4.

*Group problem-solving*

Group problem-solving was introduced in several cases. In certain instances this was adopted in order to increase job scope and team spirit. In other cases the aim was the smooth implementation of change. In Case 5 a staff meeting was held to enable staff in a sales accounting department to contribute ideas on ways of improving the work organisation. Whilst action points emerged from this meeting and changes resulted there were no follow-up meetings for some considerable time. Staff seemed unsure about the objectives for the meeting, seeing it as an opportunity for the manager to collect information. Following the six-month review of the change programme, follow-up meetings were planned. Whilst the manager in Case 6 planned to hold a staff meeting at the workshop to explore problems, on return to work one of the supervisors questioned staff informally. No reason for the change in strategy was provided. Regular monthly staff meetings were held in this department prior to the workshop.

*Involvement in planning change*

Staff were involved in planning the implementation of change in several cases. Decisions to implement changes were in each of these cases made prior to the workshop and by managers more senior to those present. Staff, however, were involved in detailed decisions about such aspects as work organisation (Cases 2 and 7), office layout (Case 7) and the final selection of equipment (Cases 8 and 9).

In the reprographics department of Case 9 the staff were reported as being involved successully in decisions about equipment suitability, whereas in Case 8 the supervisor reported little success. Two reasons were established for this apparent failure. Initially staff had limited knowledge about equipment other than that with which they were familiar. Secondly, the supervisor appeared reluctant to give them access to the information and encouragement to develop their knowledge. The involvement of staff in planning changes was seen as particularly successful in Cases 2 and 7. In both the time scale for implementing the changes had been extended, largely as the result of technical problems, but also in Case 7 as the result of inability to influence user departments.

### Group tasks

Teams were assigned a complete task in two cases. Sub-groups were formed in Case 4 with responsibility for all functions relating to a section of the alphabet. One older worker, after initial enthusiasm, had difficulty adjusting and a special task was created for her. Otherwise the system worked well for a short period. A major reorganisation occurred and during the 'crisis' period the manager decided to return to the former organisation. It was planned to introduce work groups as new staff became familiar with the jobs. A team emphasis was developed in Case 6, with each team assigned a complete task. This aroused concern elsewhere in the organisation and was curtailed because the finance department considered it to be a security risk. Staff involved were very unsettled by the return to more narrowly defined roles which seemed no longer to meet their expectations.

### Improved feedback

Where clerks were involved in resolving queries they obtained direct feedback about their own work (Cases 1 and 6). Whilst problems resulted in Case 6, the other example appeared to have been successful. Involvement in resolving problems of this type could also result in clerks developing a better understanding of the total work process. In Case 9 clerks were given appreciation training in order to increase their understanding of the total organisation and their role within it. In Case 5 visits to remote locations were planned for clerks. Time and cost appeared to have been limiting factors. In another case, a visit to a remote location was seen by the manager as a form of reward substituting for financial gain.

## Developing new skills

For older general clerks with no promotional opportunities the manager in Case 9 decided to stimulate interest by involving them in training younger clerks. This was particularly successful for one person. Opportunities to learn jobs outside the department were made available in Case 8. Again one person was reported as having benefited considerably from the programme.

## Changing recruitment practices

Discussions at the workshop about the nature of the work led the manager in Case 1 to consider recruitment practices. Opportunities for changing the nature of work were very limited and it became apparent that a better match between needs of the job-holder and the work available was possible to achieve by changing recruitment practices. Formerly staff were encouraged to train for membership of a professional institute. Many of the clerks had the necessary 'A' level passes in the UK General Certificate of Education. They appeared bored by the work after a short period. Reconsideration of recruitment practices produced positive results. Similar consideration was to be given by the manager in Case 5.

## Changing supervisory style

The situation in Case 8 where the supervisor appeared reluctant to involve staff in equipment selection has already been described. This particular supervisor had attended the workshop. In Case 5, the manager, prior to the workshop, had been encouraging the supervisor to delegate more work and also to give clerks a wider job training. At the workshop the manager decided to involve the supervisor in bringing about changes in the department including increased levels of computerisation. The manager delegated more work to the supervisor in order to encourage him to release some of the more routine elements to the clerks. Six months following these changes the supervisor still dealt with a large number of queries, tending to regard the staff as inexperienced. He preferred to deal directly with queries rather than giving the staff the explanation necessary to enable them to carry out the task. Whilst staff were handling more queries, some appeared lacking in experience and confidence and tended to rely upon the supervisor. Without a change in the supervisor's approach the rate of progress in developing staff is likely to be slow.

*Modified action plans*

Some of the action plans formulated at the workshop underwent considerable change. In Case 4 the manager had identified three aspects for change. On return to his office he held a meeting with staff to discuss the plan and possibilities and staff expressed enthusiasm and agreed to proceed. The new system developed and implemented was based on the formation of sub-groups, an aspect not included in the original plan. In this case, as in Case 6, changes outside the control of the manager led to curtailment of the project. In both cases the manager appeared to have considered the job redesign exercise in isolation from other changes in the company. This may reflect ignorance of impending changes even though they had a significant impact upon his own job and that of subordinates.

Consideration, when planning change, must be given to the implications of actions for other parts of the organisation. In Case 6 the eventual outcomes indicate lack of foresight about the implications. In Case 7 consideration of the implications appeared to be leading to hesitancy in implementation. Clearly the timing of actions will have considerable impact on the success of a change project.

External influences not anticipated at the time of the workshop were identified by several managers. In Case 3 a reduction in the department's workload removed much of the pressure for change as perceived by the manager (at the first workshop increased workload was expected). The personal problems experienced by the senior clerk in this case seem to have influenced her willingness to delegate work. The departure of the O&M assistant in Case 9 made possible a re-allocation of work including administrative work. In Case 2 one clerk failed her external examinations, a factor contributing to lowered morale. Also a job evaluation exercise did not meet expectations. The particular department was seen by the manager as having experienced too much change. Events not anticipated can offer opportunities to implement changes but the manager needs to have clear overall objectives if such opportunities are to be used effectively.


*Scope of change*

Each of the projects described in this section may be seen as successful in part in achieving the objectives set by the managers concerned. The actions proposed by some managers were within the scope of their own authority. Implementation was not dependent upon achieving the agreement of superiors or user departments. Changes were implemented with the agreement of subordinates or possibly further diagnosis and planning carried out by subordinates. The managers involved reported a high degree of success in achieving objectives. The views of subordinates about the degrees of success in one case particularly differed from the manager.

Where changes proposed depended upon the agreement of parties outside the section or department success was less apparent. In Case 6 a failure to consult other interested parties appeared to have contributed to the lack of consideration of the security implications of the changes introduced. The introduction of changes in departments outside the direct responsibility of the manager (Case 7) presented particular problems. Whilst in one department a satisfactory work organisation was being developed, other managers had not yet been convinced of the merits of the overall reorganisation proposed.

*Lack of change*

In three cases, little evidence was available about the situation following the workshop. In two cases the participants reported no change (Cases 10 and 11). The introduction of computer facilities had been delayed in Case 10. Even so the actions proposed to prepare for their introduction had not been pursued. In Case 11 an O&M officer had moved to a different job and the project was not developed. In Case 12 the training manager indicated that progress had been made in resolving the difficulties but failed to report on the developments. In both Cases 11 and 12 the participant was only able to act in an advisory capacity regarding the implementation of change. Whilst in many organisations staff in similar functions may have considerable influence over change this was not apparant in these two situations.

**Conclusions**

Here we will summarise the more general points which can be concluded from the nine projects where changes were implemented.

Several projects would have been more successful had more effort been expended at the planning stage. At this stage identification of likely barriers to implementation and prediction of the implications of alternative courses of action would have increased the likelihood of successful implementation. The strategies developed for introducing changes would then have probably been more comprehensive and included contingency plans. Estimation of the resources required to implement change may have led in some cases to less ambitious plans and, in others, attempts to obtain suitable resources.

Where problems of employee motivation following technological change were apparent, the changes which appear to have been most successfully implemented were those feasible within the authority of the manager concerned. For example, where the skills demanded by the new job were diminished, the manager set up projects within his department as a means for developing skills and experience. It appeared also to increase job interest. The degree of success, however, depended upon the manager's ability to identify suitable problems for investigation and his tutoring skills, as well as the clerk's enthusiasm and capabilities. Sufficient slack resource has to be made available in the department to provide the time necessary for such work. Positive benefits in terms of increased efficiency were shown to have resulted.

An approach similar to project work involving individual and group problem-solving was also used as a means for improving the nature of the work. Associated new responsibilities did not appeal to all the staff, support for the individual being vital during the period needed to build confidence. The group problem-solving resulted, in one case particularly, in creative and workable solutions to the problems being experienced.

Managers embarking upon work reorganisation found that they had new demands placed upon them. The acceptability to staff of change appears to have been influenced by the manager's style and approach. The manager's own drive and enthusiasm also appears to have considerably affected the degree to which changes were implemented. The willingness of the supervisor to modify his approach to managing was tested in several cases. Where tasks are to be delegated, the supervisor has not only to accept the rationale for the changes and the nature of changes proposed, but he must also be prepared to invest his own time in developing the knowledge, skills and confidence of staff. Where group problem-solving was adopted for planning change, managers had to make information available for progress to result. In these circumstances the manager was not in a position to control the outcomes to the same extent as in a non-participative decision-making process. Some of the managers appeared to have experienced difficulty with this style of management.

The development of the skills necessary to perform a range of tasks at work was a focal point in several projects. A flexible and adaptable workforce appeared to have several benefits from a management viewpoint. Staff seemed to develop a better understanding of the total work process through performing all the associated tasks, hence one may expect that improved individual and group performance resulted. The implementation of change is likely to be less traumatic if staff have a wide range of skills and the ability to adapt. Developing flexibility and multi-skills, however, demands training resources and the cost implications of this have to be considered.

Earlier we referred to individuals who did not seek increased responsibility. In several of the cases investigated some staff did not wish the level of responsibility in their jobs to be changed. In one case a special job was developed for the one older worker who experienced difficulty in adapting. The older workers in another case became involved in training young staff. Project work was only assigned to career-orientated staff in another case.

Staff expectations were found to have been raised during the planning and implementation of change. Equipment difficulties in several cases prolonged the implementation phase. Consequently, staff had to perform additional duties over a prolonged period. The equipment also failed to meet expectations in one case due to system inadequacies. This built in additional frustration for staff. Expectations were created during a staff meeting in one case. Whilst uncertainty about the purpose of the meeting existed, a lack of follow-up discussions resulted in unfulfilled expectations and disappointment.

Clearly, the manager in these cases was responsible for managing the changes. He was required to decide the objectives to be achieved; what change, if any, was appropriate; the rate of implementing change. The evaluation of the effectiveness of change will be related to the objectives established within the overall aims of his area of responsibility. Regular monitoring led in several cases to rethink about the direction of the changes.

Whilst we presented to participants a framework for examining the design of jobs and work group activity, participants decided for themselves the nature of the problems in their own work area. The evidence presented here appears to support the relevance of these design principles. The principles, however, related to one aspect of the total job and the context in which it is carried out. Where motivational problems exist a mismatch between individual needs and the job may exist. The solution, however, may lie in one or more of several directions, e.g. changing recruitment policies and practices, in automating the process or in changing the nature of the work and its organisation. The manager exercises his skill in diagnosing problems, deciding what to change and how, implementing change and monitoring ongoing progress.

---

**SUMMARY POINTS**

1   Change in the technologies used often results in motivational problems which have to be tackled following implementation by the line manager, as illustrated in many of our cases.

2   By anticipating motivational problems at the design stage and then careful planning many of these problems will be avoided.

3   Identify alternative ways of organising work at the design stage and select the most appropriate.

4    In selecting a method of organising work consider staff needs and expectations as well as management's objectives.

5    Staff involvement in planning change will often result in improved implementation.

6    Managers with responsibility for introducing change must be given the necessary authority.

# CHAPTER 6

# *Health, safety and ergonomic aspects of workplace design*

In the three previous chapters we have considered orgnaisational aspects in the modern office. We now turn to an area that has been the focus of much attention during the last few years: health, safety and the ergonomic aspects of workplace design. We shall examine some of the issues relating to both equipment design and workplace layout, and highlight particular areas that warrant the careful consideration of decision-makers. Many of the points made relate to offices using conventional equipment as well as those employing computer-based technologies but particular emphasis is placed upon the latter.

Visual display units in the office, particularly, present new problems for those designing workplaces. Inadequate design can lead to operators feeling excessively fatigued and stressed. The long-term impact on staff of poorly designed equipment and work-layout is less certain. What can be stated with a degree of certainty is that the consequence of poor design is greater inefficiency overall. The additional cost and time involved in applying the principles of good workplace design are usually insignificant when compared with the total cost of the system and its operation.

In the three previous chapters we have seen something of differences in the ways in which individuals are motivated. When considering health and safety and ergonomic aspects we are again dealing with individuals who will vary in their responses. Some people will be more susceptible than others to physical problems such as eye strain. Again we are looking at an area of investigation where evidence is not conclusive. However, based on the available research evidence, it is possible to formulate 'recommendations for good practice'.

Whilst complaints about mental and physical fatigue resulting from using office equipment are difficult to quantify, it is generally accepted that certain factors contribute to fatigue. In this chapter we will consider factors such as visual discomfort, postural discomfort, personal aspects, environmental aspects and task requirements.

## Visual discomfort

Visual and general discomfort and fatigue can result from problems associated with the design of visual display units (VDUs), keyboards, other work surfaces and the presentation of source documents. Of particular concern are some of the effects of working constantly with VDUs. In most systems the VDU plays a central role facilitating operators in checking input, communicating with the system, etc. Work effectiveness and operator comfort will depend upon both the legibility and readability of the display.

The legibility of individual characters on the screen influences the operator's ability to detect and discriminate between these characters. Readability is influenced by the spacing of characters and words. Factors influencing legibility include size, resolution, brightness and contrast and the similarities of shape and construction. The most commonly confused alphanumeric characters are 1 and I, 2 interpreted as Z, B interpreted as R, S or 8. Clearly the greater the similarity between characters the greater the risk of error or confusion. The height and spacing of characters and the spacing of rows of characters will all affect legibility and readability.

Most systems are equipped to store more text than can be displayed on the screen at any one time. This display memory has to be accessible, the process of retrieval to the screen being described as 'scrolling'. For example, vertical scrolling can be based on the movement of text up and down the screen (roll scrolling) or alternatively page scrolling can be available (page-by-page display). Here the response time can be an important consideration and affect both output and the operator's feelings of frustration.

The flicker which can be perceived on VDUs is the result of the constant refreshing of the phosphor which produces the characters. The 'flicker' phenomenon is part of the wider aspect of image stability. Other factors influence image stability, such as fluctuations in the power supply to the terminal and the synchronisation of the line scanning. Excessive image instability will lead to visual discomfort for the operator.

Many operators prefer yellow/green characters on a darker green background and this preference is supported by much expert opinion. This combination is believed to ensure good character readability, good overall contrast and preserves the life of the cathode ray tube. However, there is not complete consensus, since white characters on a black background give good legibility and contrast with less glare than other combinations. Contrast on the VDU screen will be affected by the general level of illumination at the workplace. Source documents also have to be illuminated and a compromise has to be sought between general levels of illumination and glare on VDU screens. Contrast control on VDUs is important in order that operators can make adjustments to suit themselves. Contrast glare resulting when VDUs are viewed against the background of a bright window or well-lit and light-coloured walls can also contribute to visual discomfort and eye strain. Anti-glare screens and low-glare non-reflecting glass can reduce the problem. Well designed office lighting can also assist.

When considering visual discomfort it is necessary also to examine the keyboard. Reflections from the keyboard result when the shape and texture of the key surface is inappropriate; visual discomfort can result when the key legends are illegible through wear, or poor design. If the distance of the keyboard is fixed and different from that of both screen and source document this will demand additional eye adjustment.

For a well trained operator the legibility of keys should not affect performance. Accuracy in keyboarding has been found to be greater where audible feedback of depression is provided. Other important factors are the force needed to depress keys, key travel, shape, and size and spacing.

The quality of source documents should also be considered. Poor legibility will result in high error rates, stress and poorer quality work. Comments about illumination have been made earlier. Document holders are useful in presenting the information at a suitable angle and height.

## Postural factors

Sitting position has a considerable influence over feelings of fatigue or stress at work. Fatigue symptoms including visual fatigue may be the result of poor working posture. Two aspects need to be taken into account when designing workplaces and diagnosing workplace problems, i.e.

1    Awkward posture being adopted to compensate for poor workplace design, visual factors and unadjustable furniture.
2    Fixed posture where one working position has to be adopted for long periods during work.

The design of the workplace must consider the position and freedom of movement required by the hands, arms, legs and head, as well as the appropriateness of the viewing distances involved whilst working with the equipment. Work should be organised so as to avoid, wherever possible, long periods in a static working position.

The first stage in designing systems or diagnosing problems is to identify the nature of the tasks to be performed. On VDU systems the work normally falls into one of three general categories, i.e. data input, dialogue-type tasks and data enquiry. In the first category the operator is mainly engaged in reading information from a written document or translating information from audio equipment and then keying it into the computer terminal. Dialogue-type tasks involve the transfer of information from either the source document or a person to the computer and *vice vesa*. The third category, data enquiry, involves requesting information from the computer. The emphasis varies in these three work situations in the extent to which it requires reading/listening to source information, keyboard and keyboarding skills, observing the screen, skills in accessing data. When compromises have to be taken in applying the principles of good workplace design the nature of the work should be considered and emphasis placed upon ensuring that factors most likely to be problematic are dealt with. However, the keyboard and keyboarding skills are predominant.

The most important general considerations are that the operator can work in a comfortable position, can move in and out of the workplace with ease, can see and read the various documents and screens, can reach and operate with ease the controls in constant use and has easy access to equipment which is used less frequently. There must also be adequate desk space to enable incoming and outgoing work to be stored, documents to be perused, etc.

The principles of good ergonomic practice are illustrated in Exhibit 16, which shows their application in the design of a VDU workplace.

Where problems are evident at the workplace it is necessary to bear in mind during investigation that the symptoms of poor posture including backache, eye strain, headaches and general fatigue can result from inappropriate workplace design for the type of work predominating. Alternatively, these symptoms may be the result of activities outside work, or the result of the individual's psychological state and response to the work itself. Another possibility is that whilst the workplace layout is adequate the environmental conditions are not. These factors are to be considered in subsequent sections. However, two important guiding principles should be adopted in workplace design:

1   The workplace design and work organisation should encourage operators to change their working posture frequently.
2   The design of work stations should permit operators to adjust reading distance, viewing angles, seat height, etc.

### Personal aspects

Personal factors may result in greater susceptibility to fatigue. We have stressed earlier that many of the symptoms of visual discomfort amongst VDU operators are closely related to, and sometimes the direct consequence of, poor working posture and that the two problems have to be considered simultaneously. The acceleration of visual fatigue at work is likely to be the result of a combination of work-related and personal factors. These personal factors include:

1   Visual defects — previously tolerable defects may not be

86

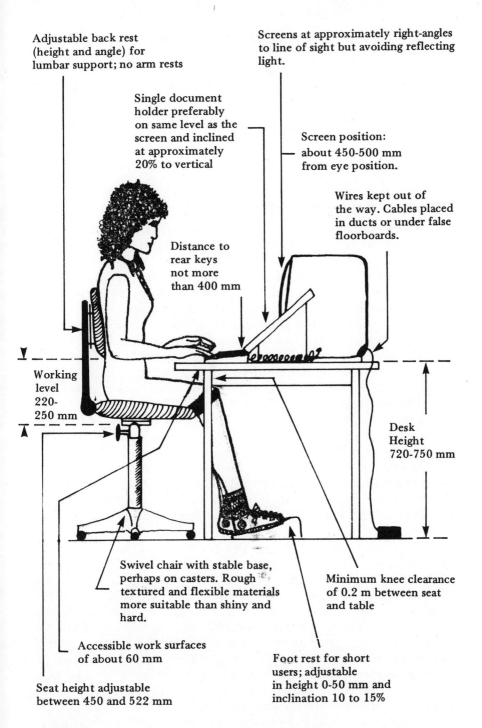

Adjustable back rest (height and angle) for lumbar support; no arm rests

Screens at approximately right-angles to line of sight but avoiding reflecting light.

Single document holder preferably on same level as the screen and inclined at approximately 20% to vertical

Screen position: about 450-500 mm from eye position.

Wires kept out of the way. Cables placed in ducts or under false floorboards.

Distance to rear keys not more than 400 mm

Working level 220-250 mm

Desk Height 720-750 mm

Swivel chair with stable base, perhaps on casters. Rough textured and flexible materials more suitable than shiny and hard.

Minimum knee clearance of 0.2 m between seat and table

Accessible work surfaces of about 60 mm

Foot rest for short users; adjustable in height 0-50 mm and inclination 10 to 15%

Seat height adjustable between 450 and 522 mm

**EXHIBIT 16**  Principles of good work-station design

87

acceptable when working with VDUs. Special eye-tests may be necessary, and are advised in situations where employees will be using VDUs for long periods.

2 Personal health — tiredness, general poor health, smoking, drinking, etc. Epileptics are prone to suffer seizures when watching television and consequently working with VDUs may be ill-advised. Medical advice should be sought in such cases.

3 Age.

4 Adoption of poor working posture.


## Environmental factors

In this section we will consider four environmental factors, i.e. lighting, temperature, noise and space. Lighting is probably the most important consideration with reference particularly to VDU workplaces. Nevertheless, electrical equipment may produce heat which can lead to discomfort if not considered at the design stage. Some items of equipment in the office are noisy, particularly printers.

The quality of illumination of the item being read and the difficulty of the visual task affect the ease of character recognition. Some aspects have already been considered, e.g. screen contrasts. No hard and fast rules are available to the lighting designer although some general observations can be made. High levels of illumination can be as unacceptable to operators as low levels. This will be the case particularly where there are problems of glare from VDU screens. The main factors contributing to glare are the power of light sources, positioning of light sources relative to lines of vision and screen, the direction of light sources and the reflective properties of the various items of furniture and decor in the office. Glare shields can be used to overcome the problems of both direct and reflective glare. Another factor to be attended to with regard to visual fatigue is the variation in levels of illumination between frequently used surfaces.

Further important considerations when designing the office are the ambient temperature and frequency of air changes. The combined effect of thermal emission from equipment must be taken into account when designing heating and air conditioning systems. Draughts are probably a greater source of operator complaint than the overall ambient temperature. Dry environments also contribute to visual and more general operator fatigue; therefore, the relative humidity should also be assessed.

Noise sources within the office include line-printers, copiers, fans, typewriters and conversations. External noise can result from nearby road traffic, traffic within the building, building services, etc. Noise can be distracting and lead to a reduction in operator performance due to interrupted concentration causing irritability and stress. A lack of noise

---

**A CASE EXAMPLE OF ENVIRONMENTAL PROBLEMS**

Two operators using a minicomputer (with screens) complained of nausea and vertigo. There was a considerable amount of sick leave (mostly uncertified) and one operator eventually resigned. Although the other was prepared to stay, there were problems in attracting internal recruits to transfer to the work. At this point, the manager sought help. Could it be the screens? Enquiries revealed:

- The operators were required to do clerical work as well as use the machines.
- There was little work surface but many papers.
- Source documents were poor.
- The room was only just large enough for the machines.
- The door was closed because of the girls' wish to work uninterrupted.
- There were windows but these were not used and in fact the blinds were kept drawn because of light falling onto the screen.
- Artificial light was poor and not well placed for working.
- The walls were painted cream and reflected light onto the screens.
- There was no air conditioning and no ventilation from above.

By this time the manager recognised the problems were not just caused by the machines and he sought co-operation from an environmental specialist in the company.

Ultimately, the room was redesigned to provide adequate ventilation, lighting was corrected and the room was redecorated to avoid reflection. The work mix was checked and amended, i.e. the job was improved to give variety and contact outside the room.

The new arrangements seem to have been satisfactory.

---

**EXHIBIT 17**   A case example of environmental problems

can also be disturbing. Again a compromise has to be sought. Noise levels can be reduced significantly by good equipment selection, the materials used in decor design, the use of acoustic hoods over equipment, and absorbant supports for equipment subject to vibration.

Many of the problems of noise and excessive heat generation can be overcome by giving adequate consideration to the space availability in the office, the layout of the equipment, screens and plants. Another important aspect to take into account when designing office layout is the personal space afforded to operators. As was stressed in earlier chapters, opportunities to interact with colleagues are important. However, people have a need for 'personal space' and a degree of separation from others as well as space in which they can work with a degree of privacy.

In Exhibit 17 we have described a brief case example to illustrate some of the problems that can arise due to poor environmental design. In this particular case it would appear that the VDU screens were not, as thought initially, the main source of problems.

## Task requirements

The performance of individual operators will be influenced by factors such as the pace of work, the degree of continuous work, the variation in activity, the concentration demands and the extent of unwelcomed interruptions. Performance will also be affected by the frequency and duration of rest periods. The ability of individuals to perform well will vary considerably and the response to rest periods will also be different.

Tasks differ in the extent to which intense activity may or may not be interspersed between pauses awaiting response. Frequent changes of activity stimulate high performance from some operators, whereas for others they break a work rhythm. Research evidence exists suggesting that frequent rest pauses taken before high levels of fatigue occur are more effective than longer but less frequent pauses following a drop in performance. When considering overall productivity, pause times of between 5 and 10 per cent of the total working time are normally compensated by the recuperating affects of the pauses. Again, however, there are no hard and fast rules. Many jobs, anyway, permit people to regulate their own rate of working throughout the day, taking pauses at discretion. Official break periods may then not be as essential for the purpose of recuperation.

---

### SUMMARY POINTS

1 Excessive fatigue and stress can result from poor equipment and workplace design. In turn overall efficiency will be reduced.

2 Avoid where possible factors contributing to visual discomfort — poorly designed or ineffective equipment, inadequate illumination, glare, illegible source documents and long periods of concentrated activity.

3 Postural discomfort results from poorly designed workplaces and tasks organised such that little change in working position is permitted. Ensure that equipment can be adjusted by operators for their own comfort.

4 Eye-tests are advised when selecting VDU operators. Medical problems, especially epilepsy, should also be checked.

5 Environmental design will affect operator performance. Lighting, temperature, humidity, noise and general layout should all be considered.

6 Greater productivity can result when operators have discretion to take rest-periods when they begin to feel tired rather than at fixed intervals.

# CHAPTER 7

# *Introducing changes in the office*

Much of the earlier part of the book has been devoted to a consideration of 'good practice' in the design of jobs, work group organisation and the workplace. Whilst we have touched upon the approaches adopted for introducing change, up to this point we have not considered the change process in detail.

From previous chapters we can draw conclusions about the type of problems experienced in managing offices where new technology has been introduced with minimal consideration of the human aspects of the system prior to its operation. The problems resulting have had to be tackled at a later stage by the manager responsible for the area affected and there has been a general acceptance of the technology and systems as designed. We have also described several cases where attempts were made to anticipate the implications of new technology for staff involved, well in advance of its operation.

It has also been stressed that there is no 'recipe book' solution to be applied where problems are being experienced. In fact, management tasks, in such circumstances, may be compared to those of the medical practitioner in that he needs to:

1   Identify the symptoms of disease apparent in the situation.
2   Diagnose the disease or cause of trouble.
3   Decide how it might be dealt with, i.e. make selections from the possible treatments.
4   Start the treatment.
5   Monitor developments and take corrective steps where necessary.

As in the case of medicine, the emphasis can be remedial or it can be preventive. Problems can be tackled as they arise following the implementation or attempted implementation of new technologies and systems. Alternatively, attention can be paid to planning acceptable jobs, work group organisation and workplace design during the decision-making process, a deliberate attempt being made at each stage to achieve the 'best fit' between technological and social needs.

Whether changes are to be introduced for preventive or remedial reasons it is apparent from the case material considered earlier that great care is needed in preparation and introduction. In this chapter we will start by looking in more detail at how to plan and implement change generally. We will carry out further analysis of the case material to support points being made. This will be followed by consideration of practical means for integrating technical and social objectives in the design of new work systems.

## Stages in a change process

Managers and staff are not unused to changes at work, focusing on possibly technology, organisation or managerial style. Change, in some instances, will undoubtedly have been planned carefully, whereas others will have been the result of chance occurrences. Reflection on these experiences (successes, failures, missed opportunities, problems) can provide a useful set of guidelines for consideration when faced with new challenges.

Even when planned, organisational change clearly does not proceed in an orderly step-wise manner. Since, however, for our purposes here we need to describe change, whether in persons, groups or organisations, we must for the purpose of illustration identify stages in the process of introducing change. At the same time we must not overlook the cyclic nature of change in practice, and also that many activities will be taking place simultaneously. Steps in the process of planned change are illustrated in Exhibit 18. The arrows have been drawn to indicate both the main direction in the process as well as the iterative nature of the process in which at any stage there may be a return to previous stages, e.g. goals may need further clarification when changes are being planned.

### Stage 1  Awareness of the need for change

The first stage in the process is awareness that change is needed either to remedy existing problems or in response to changing needs. This awareness may be aroused by symptoms such as high labour turnover, absenteeism or low productivity or it may result from the development of more efficient technologies and the need to maintain competitiveness. An awareness of the existence of a problem is not automatically translated into a desire for change. Often members of organisations avoid tackling problems in the hope that they will just disappear. In our earlier discussion of expectancy theory (Chapter 4), we noted the ideas of expectancy and valence. It was suggested that people would be more

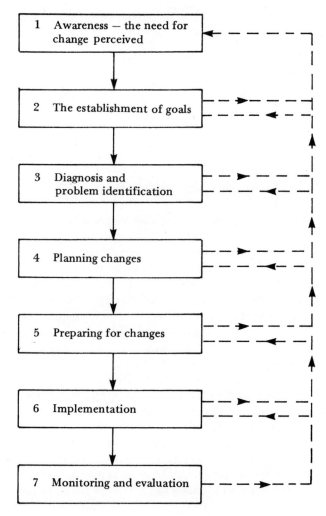

**EXHIBIT 18**   Steps in the process of planned change

positively motivated where they had a preference for attaining a particular outcome and an expectation that the outcome would result from a particular course of action. It appears then, that unless there is some confidence that the problem is capable of solution and a better state of affairs is attainable, people are unlikely to commit themselves to a change effort.

### Stage 2   Establishing goals

Problems will be defined in different ways depending on the individual's goals and preferences, e.g. to management technological changes may

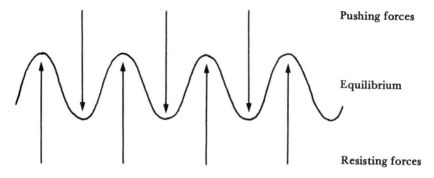

Pushing forces

Equilibrium

Resisting forces

**EXHIBIT 19**   The balancing forces for change

represent improved efficiency but to employees may be seen as likely to reduce job opportunities. Different interest groups will assess the likelihood of their own goals being achieved and seek advantage in terms relevant to their own needs. For progress to be made in planning changes it is necessary to define the goals to be achieved. The various parties may have differing goals but sufficient points of common interest have to be found in order to commence the planning process. Resistance to change may come from many sources. People's attitudes to change are influenced considerably by previous experiences, expectations concerning the likely costs and benefits, the amount of personal effort they expect to be demanded of them. Additionally, there is often a reluctance to admit the need for both change and assistance from others since this may be contrued as an admission of one's own inability to manage the situation effectively.

A useful and simple method for illustrating the various forces influencing change is that developed by Kurt Lewin* based on his idea of 'field theory'. Any situation can be seen as in temporary equilibrium with the forces acting to change the situation being balanced by the forces acting to resist the change. This is illustrated in the simple diagram in Exhibit 19. In carrying out an analysis using this approach the first step is to write down the problem and the parties involved. The next stage involves establishing one's own objectives. Following this all the factors currently pushing in the direction of change should be listed, then all the restraining forces. These forces will include the policies and procedures as well as outside pressures. The forces should then be given a rating: high, medium or low. The diagram can then be constructed with arrows varying in length to represent the strength of the various forces. An example is shown in Exhibit 20. This form of 'mapping' can assist in identifying the goals of the various parties, areas where common interests exist and pressures resisting change. This analysis can be an aid also at later stages in the process of planned change.

*Lewin, K., *Field Theory in Social Science*, Harper (1951).

94

MANAGER'S PROBLEM: *The introduction of word processing systems**

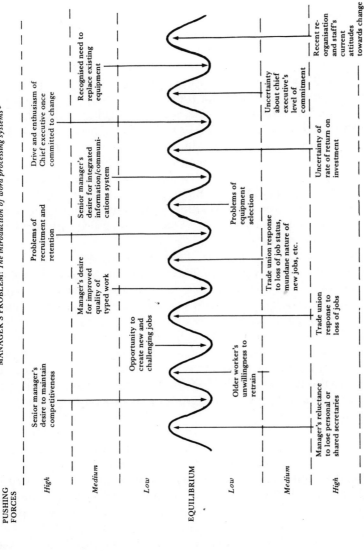

*Some of these issues appeared in Case 7.

**EXHIBIT 20** A partial illustration of force field analysis

*Stage 3    Diagnosis and problem identification*

The next stage in the change process as illustrated in Exhibit 18 is the diagnostic phase. This stage involves the analysis of the situation in order to check the symptoms of the problem and to identify the causes. Where implementation of new technologies is being planned it is often necessary and usually worthwhile to examine existing solutions in order that mistakes are not repeated and that basic information about the existing solutions is available for effective planning to be carried out.

When examining a situation where problems are thought to exist the investigator will compare the situation as found with some ideal. The investigator will have a concept for framework on how an organisation should operate. Each of us has such a concept, varying in the extent of sophistication and relation to reality or its validity. This concept will be modified over time, influenced by discussion and experiences.

The final diagnosis may well be improved by involving people with wide-ranging interests, different views of 'good organisation' and a variety of specialist knowledge. Each person, in bringing his own perspective, will view the situation differently and by combining in the investigation the final analysis will be broader and reflect the views of a wider range of interested parties.

The approach most appropriate for diagnosing the problems will vary between situations. A preliminary diagnosis may be based on scant information and be undertaken by the manager personally. More detailed studies may be assigned to working parties who then collect information through attitude surveys, interview programmes, method study, etc. Clearly the approach has to be tailored to the situation. In the small organisation discussion may take place with all the staff in a relatively informal manner and consensus be reached about action. In the larger organisation established machinery may exist for consultation or participation and representative groups may be assigned to the task. The methods to be used will have to be related also to the nature of the problem being investigated, e.g. where labour turnover is high an analysis of reasons for leaving would be useful. The extent of awareness of the need for change, the extent to which a solution to the problem is critical to the continuance of the organisation and the urgency of solution will also influence the choice of approach to problem diagnosis.

Two key questions must be answered in this diagnosistic stage: whether or not to proceed with a change strategy and how to proceed. Earlier we identified four areas of focus for change effort: task, technology, structure, people. In this book we have concentrated upon three of these areas: the task to be performed in the form of jobs, the structure in the shape of work organisation and the technology. Diagnosis then must consider both the technical and operational aspects of the work as well as the social and psychological needs of the individuals involved. The diagnosis should consider also the wider aspects of employee relations with the company, e.g. personnel policies, training, communications and information systems, decision-making procedures and reward systems and levels. Broadening the diagnosis one could include consideration of the task to be performed (how essential is it?) and the people (what interpersonal conflict exists within and between groups?). The diagnosis of problems will only be as valid as the information upon which that diagnosis is based. The focus for change, the point of intervention, has to be chosen from task, technology, structure and people.

In Chapter 4, we suggested that many problems seemed to be circular in nature (see Exhibit 6, page 30).

Analysis of the case studies supported this view. In many instances the problems included in Exhibit 7 (page 31) had multiple causes. One problem seemed to lead to further secondary problems as predictable from Exhibit 6. In consequence the actions proposed often included several different interventions aimed at achieving improvement (Exhibit 8, p 35). Actions proposed in several cases involved measures aimed at changing the people, e.g. changes in recruitment practices to better match people and jobs, involvement of supervision and staff in joint problem-solving aimed at changing supervisory styles. In Case 7, new technology was being adopted partially to overcome problems of staff recruitment and retention. In Case 1, the manager would have welcomed improvements in technology and systems to reduce the frustration resulting from slow computer response. In other cases the structure of jobs and the work organisation was the main focus of changes. Whatever the focus of change, a systematic approach to problem diagnosis seems particularly important. A systematic approach, with well kept records, can assist at a later stage in the change process by facilitating monitoring and evaluation.

When deciding which route to take it is necessary to weigh up not only the likelihood of the change solving the problem but also the likelihood of successful implementation. The following criteria are important for consideration when selecting from alternative courses of action:

1   Technically feasible (it must look as though it would work).
2   Social and political acceptability (those in a position of power are likely to accept the proposals).
3   Economically viable (that it can be achieved within the current pay-back criteria for investment and that it will prove cost-effective in operation).
4   Administratively convenient and organisationally feasible (it is presented in a way consistent with existing procedures and practices in the organisation).

The need for detailed planning of the change programme was emphasised in both Chapters 3 and 5. Two brief case examples in Chapter 3 illustrated different approaches to planning change. The first case in the data preparation department of a manufacturing company used a highly structured process for planning change. A management working party was responsibile for formulating proposals and monitoring their implementation. In the second case, the management and staff in a local office of a Civil Service Department jointly planned change. In both cases successful outcomes were reported.

Involvement of staff in planning change was adopted in several cases reported in the case studies. The outcomes of the planning process were different to those envisaged by management, particularly in Case 5. The reasons for staff involvement in the process included the intention of making jobs more interesting by greater involvement in planning change; an attempt to influence the supervisory style; the objective of gaining greater commitment to the change programme; to create enthusiasm for the change and in turn smoother implementation. Particularly in Case 5, the involvement of staff in change planning had beneficial effects as far as management was concerned. However, in this particular case the feelings of staff were less positive about the involvement since they were unsure of the purpose of the participative process. Certainly, participative planning can increase staff frustration where change is slow or fails to materialise. Also where large departments are concerned the participative process, for practical reasons, may involve staff representatives and thus direct participation is very limited.

Participative approaches to planning change seemed to be effective within the boundaries of the area for which the manager involved had responsibility. This is illustrated by reference to Cases 6 and 7. In the latter, staff decided their own work organisation but only within the office arrangements established by decisions taken at an earlier stage. Higher-level decisions remained unquestioned. In Case 6, established systems and procedures limited the choice available for the redesign of jobs and work organisation. Also here, conditions imposed by interested parties outside the area where changes were being introduced prohibited changes seen as desirable by the local staff.

Participative approaches to planning change were not used in all the case studies. In Case 3 the manager clarified his own long-term objectives and preferred organisation, then adopted an opportunistic approach to implementing change. When circumstances arose which were favourable he introduced changes in incremental stages. In Case 8 staff were involved in some change decisions but not others, and at the discretion of the manager. Staff involvement proved to be unsatisfactory from the staff's point of view because the manager did not make available information relevant to the decisions.

Projects reported in the case studies were often undertaken in relatively small sections or departments. In some instances, a high proportion of the clerical employees in the organisation were involved, in others only few. Whilst wider adoption of change was not envisaged at the outset of these projects, strategies should be identified at the planning stage where wider diffusion is sought.

The changes that appeared to have been most successfully implemented were those feasible within the authority of the manager involved. Where the agreement of more senior managers or those responsible for other departments was necessary, success in achieving the initial objectives was lower. One clear lesson to emerge was that those parties from whom agreements need to be sought must be identified early and agreement sought during the planning phase.

Forecasts about the time required to successfully implement technological change in several cases were over-optimistic. Delays resulted from technical and software problems rather than organisational and personal difficulties. In one case, however, slow progress in implementing organisational change appeared to be the result of reluctance on the part of the managers to accept change. Another feature was that delays in implementation appeared to result in staff performing additional duties for prolonged periods. There was also in several instances an underestimation of the resources required to implement change within the organisation.

Consideration when planning changes must be given to the implications of change in other parts of the organisation, as well as the impact of changes elsewhere upon the project being planned. Alternative strategies for implementing change should be evaluated in relation to these various forces.

The planning process should result not only in detailed proposals setting out modified procedures and practices and the necessary agreement but also detailed plans for implementing changes. The action plan resulting should include sub-goals, target completion dates, resource requirements and specifications of standards to be achieved.

## Stage 5   Preparing for change

Following agreement to proceed with change, preparatory work will undoubtedly be necessary. Clearly the time needed for preparatory work will relate to the type of changes being introduced. Major new equipment may require new buildings, structural alterations or re-arrangement of existing offices. Staff will have to be recruited, selected, trained and possibly some will need redeployment. Managers and specialists will need briefing. In many instances, the development of

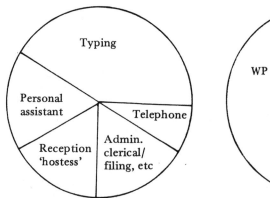

*Traditional Personal Secretary*          *WP Operator*

**EXHIBIT 21** Analysis of the jobs of personal secretary and word-processing operator

systems and software will require the most time and resource. For the office manager, however, his main concern will focus upon the preparation of staff and users.

If we take as an example a change from secretary/typists to word processing operators we can show some changes in the work which in turn will affect selection and training. An analysis of the jobs of secretary and word processing operator is likely to show a distribution of time similar to Exhibit 21. The characteristics of a good word-processing operator in consequence are likely to differ from those of a good personal secretary. One author's views of the characteristics of a successful word-processing operator are listed in Exhibit 22. Also included are the characteristics of the good supervisor, possibly a new role in the organisation. Having established the nature of the new job and the personal characteristics being sought in the job holder it is now possible to consider selection of the personnel for training. For this we need an analysis of the skills required in word processing. In a recent study* of the implementation of word processing the following skills additional to typing skills were found to be used:

1    Competence with new equipment (VDU and printer).
2    Technical understanding to manage the process.
3    Judgements, e.g. tape storage.
4    Formatting skills.
5    Problem-solving.
6    Dealing with clients (higher management in two-way traffic).
7    Patience, tact, self-control.
8    Team working.
9    Training others.

*See Hayes, F.C., 'Jobs and skills in the melting pot', *Personnel Management* (August 1979).

*A   Characteristics of a successful word-processing operator*

1   A preference for working with machines rather than with people.
2   A willingness to remain at a work situation for prolonged periods.
3   Low vulnerability to distraction by noise and activity around them.
4   Ability to work under pressure to deadlines.
5   Accustomed to close monitoring of output.
6   Ability to translate accurately from dictation.
7   Good understanding of punctuation rules.
8   Good vocabulary related to specific business operation.
9   High level of spelling ability.
10  High level of typing skills.

*B   Characteristics of a successful word-processing supervisor*

1   Prefers flexibility.
2   Enjoys change and new challenges.
3   Prefers not to be confined to one work situation.
4   Enjoys autonomy and self-organisation.
5   Possessing good 'social skills'.

**EXHIBIT 22**   Characteristics of successful word-processor operators and supervisors. *Source:* McNurlin, B.C., 'Word processing: Part 2,' *EDP Analyser* (March 1977).

Many equipment suppliers offer training facilities for those who will be supervising and operating their equipment. This training tends to focus upon the technical skills. Personal skills and attributes may need to be developed through additional training programmes, either in-company or externally.

The end-users of the new systems need to be briefed and possibly also given specialist training. Managers may well find themselves dependent upon a central administrative services unit for many of the tasks carried out by a personal or shared secretary (for example, see Case 7). This may well force the manager to organise himself better. Greater emphasis may be placed upon telephone dictation to remote equipment — a skill that needs to be developed amongst users. Users also have to be made aware of the new services available and how to make use of them.

The increasing use by managers of VDUs will lead to them needing both keyboarding skills and systems knowledge. Programming skills will also be sought by managers as they become more familiar and comfortable with new technologies and seek to better use the potential.

## Stage 6   *Implementation*

The time taken for implementing the change will depend upon the scale of the change. Installation of major new computer equipment and its commissioning will take months, possibly years. In contrast, an office reorganisation may be made on the first day of the week and adequate output maintained during the first week of operation.

Where large systems are being installed implementation is likely to be in stages. The implementation programme for software developments is likely to result in the development of complete sub-systems in each phase. Implementation of sub-systems will often affect sections of the work in various departments of the organisation simultaneously. Management in these departments will have to cope with these changes, developing methods of working for each and possibly not having a clear idea of the final form of the organisation needed to work integrated systems as yet undesigned.

The implementation of word-processing sytems in stages throughout an organisation was illustrated in Case 7. The first installations were to be a 'show piece'. By generating user interest and enthusiasm it was hoped that some of the barriers to change would be overcome. It also provided an opportunity for examination of the problems of changing to word processing — organisational, selection and training, impact on workload. These experiences should lead to better planning and smoother installation of later units. The communications department throughout this period had as an overall objective the integration of information and communications systems throughout the organisation. Therefore, they ensured that equipment was standardised and capable of eventually linking into a wider system.

Implementation in stages, in addition to developing knowledge and experience of its impact internally within the section directly involved, provides an opportunity to test back-up facilities. Particularly important amongst these back-up facilities is repair and maintenance. If the organisation is committed only to the purchase of an initial installation, equipment performance and reliability as well as the manufacturer's back-up service will obviously influence later decisions.

During implementation it is likely that dual systems will have to be maintained. Case 1 illustrated some of the frustrations experienced by clerks who were using a computer-based system during development alongside (what was to them) a more reliable and quicker manual system. In this particular case doubts were expressed by departmental staff about the likelihood of the computer department returning to complete the task and resolve the problems. The manager concerned was not in a position to question the computer programmer's technical statements about reasonable response rates.

Often staff expectations about the performance of new equipment are unrealistic. Also those responsible for selling equipment and designing systems are over-optimistic in their time estimates. Consequently a high level of tolerance is demanded from staff required to function effectively during the changeover. As was found in the case examples, resources made available to assist in change are often inadequate, particularly for

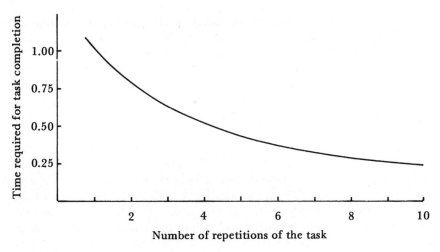

**EXHIBIT 23** A learning curve

those responsible for operating existing and new systems. The focus of attention is usually the new equipment and its operation and those who are having to keep the clerical system operating get much less attention. It is a time when co-operative working is essential.

Whilst training provided prior to implementing changes should have resulted in staff having the basic knowledge and skills required to perform the new tasks, proficiency in performance results from on-the-job practice. This performance improvement will follow a curve similar to that shown in Exhibit 23. The time required to complete a task will reduce with repeated performance but the rate of improvement will reduce over time. Task complexity, individual skills and abilities, frequency of repetition and the level of staff motivation will all affect the rate of improvement. Consequently, we would expect staff to become more proficient with experience, but continuing counselling from trainers and managers can speed up this process, a factor often overlooked.

One important role of the office manager during the implementation phase is the 'protection' of staff. During the period when staff are still learning, the manager may well find that the users of the system are making excessive demands on staff. At a time when staff are experiencing doubts about their own competence on new equipment, additional pressures from users can result in adverse staff reactions. At a time when the manager is concerned to create the impression of 'money well spent' it is important that he avoids creating too high an expectation at an early stage amongst those using the service. As staff become both competent and confident with the new equipment they will often identify additional facilities that can be made available for users. The problem facing the manager at this stage may be that of generating user awareness of, and interest in, the new facilities.

*Stage 7   Monitoring and evaluation*

An important phase in any change project, and one that often gets less attention than it ought, involves monitoring and evaluating the changes.

The criteria used for monitoring and evaluation should include the goals established for the project. These may include a reduction in operating costs to be achieved over a fixed time period, reduced staff turnover and improved staff morale. These objectives may relate to the specific project. Monitoring of wider departmental objectives should be an ongoing process. These objectives may include a specified level of customer service and overall cost targets. These indicators also may be appropriate for monitoring changes and taking corrective action when considered necessary.

Agreement about the criteria for evaluation should be established at an early stage. Data collected during the diagnostic phase may be used for comparative purposes. The evaluation itself may be carried out by management, or alternatively by a working party representing interested parties, i.e. management, specialists, staff. Where a working party was formerly responsible for planning changes it is common practice to employ the same group to undertake the project evaluation. This continuing involvement provides group members with feedback about the benefits of the changes they designed. By this means the members of the group will maximise learning from the experiences.

An important element in the evaluative process is that of providing feedback to those responsible for earlier decisions. The feedback may be about such aspects as equipment suitability, operational problems associated with new systems and procedures or the approach to implementing change.

Monitoring and evaluation, as with other stages in the change process, has to be planned. Deadline dates have to be established. Resources and time have to be made available and access to information agreed. The evaluation of change projects may be of relevance to a wider group within the organisation than those directly involved in the project and such people should be identified at an early stage and appropriate means developed for reporting the outcomes of the project. Often a verbal presentation of findings is a useful way of disseminating the experiences gained. The writing of reports is usually time-consuming and the impact is often less than that hoped for by the authors.

## Incorporating human aspects in the design process

Whilst much emphasis throughout the book has been placed on examining existing work systems where problems result from poor organisational and job design, we have stressed the benefits to be derived from designing work systems more effectively from the outset. In this section we describe how technical, operational and social needs may be more effectively considered in the design process. We do not suggest that this is the only approach that will work, but offer the suggestions to provoke discussion. The best fit between the technical, operational and social needs is only likely to be achieved where consideration is given to these aspects during the decision process. Full consideration of all aspects is unlikely unless the decision-making process is designed to facilitate representation of the various interests at each stage. Consideration of social as well as economic/technical criteria throughout the decision process is likely to result in the development of solutions different from those to be expected where more limited criteria are employed.

A recent development in many Western European countries is the concept of 'technology agreements'. The International Federation of Commerical, Clerical and Technical Employees in their 1979 publication, *Computers and Work,* advocated that trade unions should develop action programmes involving discussions with individual companies, public authorities, employers' associations, national governments, and international organisations. It is suggested that these discussions should include detailed manpower assessments, agreements about job losses and new opportunities, about the sharing of the benefits from the improved productivity, the development of new products or services and other means for maintaining employment levels as well as redundancy conditions.

In the UK, APEX* has published and widely circulated a model agreement for the introduction of new technology which is proposed as the basis for negotiations between unions and employers. This model agreement covers aspects such as job loss, reductions in the working week, joint management/union planning, job evaluation, working hours, training, health and safety and grievance/disputes procedures. The model agreement also covers access to data to enable staff representatives to monitor the impact of changes in technology.

The model technology agreement covers many aspects of new technology as they are likely to affect staff. Some organisations in the UK have reached agreement already about the implementation of specific office technology. These agreements cover many of the aspects included in the model agreement.

*APEX, *Automation and the Office Worker,* Association of Professional, Executive, Clerical and Computer Staff, London (1980).

105

One area covered by the APEX Model agreement relates to job content and job satisfaction. It advocates:

'Full analysis, through joint union/management committees, will take place in respect of the effects of new systems on job content and job satisfaction. Jobs will be carefully designed to ensure that routine and monotony are minimised.' (Clause 7, Page 58).

If these proposals are accepted a participative approach for planning change similar to that discussed earlier may become a more usual practice in organisations. This approach to the detailed design of jobs and work-group activity should go some way to ensuring that the needs of the staff are incorporated into the design process.

Technology agreements have been advocated where the impact of change could potentially affect the employment opportunities of staff. This is not always likely to be the case. The manager planning the introduction of new equipment into the office is faced with the problem of deciding who needs to be involved in agreement over what issues. He may be working in an organisation where a technology agreement has already been formulated and his proposed changes may have to be made within an existing framework. In other cases, no such agreement will exist. Nevertheless, in both instances the manager will need to assess the likely impact of the new technology and decide whose agreement to seek.

In Exhibit 24 we present an approach for assessing the impact of change and the parties to be affected. It is likely that, where changes will introduce minor improvements in office equipment as a replacement to existing, agreement will be more localised. The manager may have authority within specified limits to replace such equipment. Discussions may be held within the department and agreement reached concerning equipment type, layout and job changes. As the sophistication and extent of impact of the new equipment increases, agreement will be necessary at higher levels in the organisation, both from the more senior managers and from trade unions or staff associations. As decision-making moves up the organisation it is likely that a greater degree of formality will be present in both discussions and agreements.

Existing machinery or specially constituted groups are likely to be established to plan and agree changes where they have organisation-wide implications. In contrast where changes only impact at the local level less formal participation is possible.

However, whatever the form of the mechanism adopted for the detailed design of jobs and work-group activity, it is clear from the case studies reported earlier that no formula exists for the specification of jobs and work organisation. Each case has to be treated individually and solutions developed to meet the particular circumstances. The principles advocated in Chapter 4, whilst having general applicability,

| Level of technological change | Jobs to be affected | | | | Jobs to be reorganised | | | | Level of management agreement before implementation | | | Level of employee agreement before implementation | | |
|---|---|---|---|---|---|---|---|---|---|---|---|---|---|---|
| | IO | WG | Dep. | Org. | IO | WG | Dep. | Org. | Local | Depart-mental | Organi-sational | Local | Depart-mental | Organi-sational |
| 1   Improved equipment, e.g. more sophisticated typewriter, copier | | | | | | | | | | | | | | |
| 2   Major upgrade of existing facilities, e.g. replacement computer with increased capacity and wider application | | | | | | | | | | | | | | |
| 3   Major departures in technology or systems applications, e.g. first word processors, first mini- or mainframe computer, integration of information/communication systems | | | | | | | | | | | | | | |

IO – individual operator, WG – work group

**EXHIBIT 24** Assessing levels of technological change, their impact and parties involved

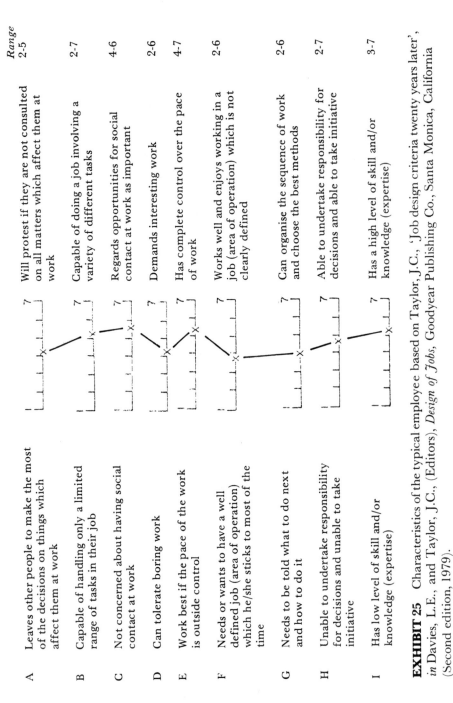

| | | Range |
|---|---|---|
| A | Leaves other people to make the most of the decisions on things which affect them at work | Will protest if they are not consulted on all matters which affect them at work | 2-5 |
| B | Capable of handling only a limited range of tasks in their job | Capable of doing a job involving a variety of different tasks | 2-7 |
| C | Not concerned about having social contact at work | Regards opportunities for social contact at work as important | 4-6 |
| D | Can tolerate boring work | Demands interesting work | 2-6 |
| E | Work best if the pace of the work is outside control | Has complete control over the pace of work | 4-7 |
| F | Needs or wants to have a well defined job (area of operation) which he/she sticks to most of the time | Works well and enjoys working in a job (area of operation) which is not clearly defined | 2-6 |
| G | Needs to be told what to do next and how to do it | Can organise the sequence of work and choose the best methods | 2-6 |
| H | Unable to undertake responsibility for decisions and unable to take initiative | Able to undertake responsibility for decisions and able to take initiative | 2-7 |
| I | Has low level of skill and/or knowledge (expertise) | Has a high level of skill and/or knowledge (expertise) | 3-7 |

**EXHIBIT 25** Characteristics of the typical employee based on Taylor, J.C., 'Job design criteria twenty years later', in Davies, L.E., and Taylor, J.C., (Editors), *Design of Jobs*, Goodyear Publishing Co, Santa Monica, California (Second edition, 1979).

| | Left statement | Scale (1–7) | Right statement | Range |
|---|---|---|---|---|
| A | Decisions on what is to be done and how it is to be done should be left entirely to management | X near 6 | Decisions should be arrived at through group discussions involving all employees | 2-7 |
| B | Job methods should be carefully defined by systems and procedures specialists, management services, or supervision | X near 4 | The development of job methods should be left to the group and individual doing the job | 1-5 |
| C | The most important motivators should be financial, e.g. high earnings and cash bonuses | X near 6 | The most important motivators should be non-financial, e.g. work challenge, opportunity for team work | 2-7 |
| D | There should be close supervision, tight controls, and well maintained discipline | X near 4 | There should be loose supervision, few controls and a reliance on employee self-discipline | 1-6 |
| E | Groups and individuals should be given the specific information they need to do the job but no more | X near 6 | Everyone should have access to all information which they regard as relevant to their work | 5-7 |
| F | Jobs should be clearly defined, structured, and stable | X near 5 | Jobs should be flexible and permit group problem-solving | 2-6 |
| G | Targets should be set by supervision and monitored by supervision | X near 4 | Targets should be left to the employee groups to set and monitor | 2-5 |
| H | There should be a clear hierarchy of authority, with the person at the top carrying ultimate responsibility for all aspects of work | X near 5 | There should be a delegation of authority and responsibility to those doing the job regardless of formal title and status | 2-6 |

**EXHIBIT 26** Ideal job characteristics and organisation structure; based on Taylor, J.C., *op. cit.* (Exhibit 25)

| Job | Availability rating | | | | |
|---|---|---|---|---|---|
| | Very low | Low | Average | High | Very high |
| **1   The design of individual jobs** | | | | | |
| Opportunity for individual to carry out varied work | | | | | |
| Non-repetitiveness of tasks | | | | | |
| Infrequency of tasks requiring attention but not being mentally absorbing | | | | | |
| Degree to which individual has discretion in task-related decision-making | | | | | |
| Extent to which individual has control over his own work | | | | | |
| The extent of well defined job objectives for the individual | | | | | |
| The extent to which achievement feedback is provided to individuals | | | | | |
| Extent to which job is 'rounded off' with visible results | | | | | |
| Extent of clear relationships between the tasks making up the job | | | | | |
| Degree to which this job relates to the total process | | | | | |
| Opportunities to interact socially with workmates at the workplace | | | | | |
| Extent to which valued skills and abilities are required | | | | | |
| **2   The design of work-group activity** | | | | | |
| Clarity in definition of work-group activity | | | | | |
| Involvement through work group in setting work targets | | | | | |
| Involvement through work group in evaluating performance | | | | | |
| Degree to which individual, through the work group, has influence over task-related decision-making | | | | | |
| Degree to which individual, through work group, is involved in non-routine decision-making | | | | | |

**EXHIBIT 27**   The design of jobs, work group activity and the workplace – a

| Job | Availability rating | | | | |
|---|---|---|---|---|---|
| | Very low | Low | Average | High | Very high |
| Degree to which group can achieve task without reliance upon others | | | | | |
| Degree of influence over those outside the work group who are needed for satisfactory task achievement | | | | | |
| 3   Equipment and workplace design | | | | | |
| Legibility and readability of any VDUs | | | | | |
| Suitability of scrolling method employed | | | | | |
| System response times | | | | | |
| Absence of flicker on VDUs | | | | | |
| Suitability of general level of illumination | | | | | |
| Absence of glare | | | | | |
| Suitability of document positioning | | | | | |
| Quality of keyboard | | | | | |
| Capacity of equipment for adjustment | | | | | |
| Suitability of posture | | | | | |
| Freedom of movement | | | | | |
| Compliance with Exhibit 16, page 87 | | | | | |
| Suitability of ambient temperature | | | | | |
| Absence of draughts | | | | | |
| Acceptability of relative humidity | | | | | |
| Acceptability of noise levels | | | | | |
| Adoption of acoustic hoods | | | | | |
| Opportunities for privacy | | | | | |
| Adequacy of storage space and flat work surfaces | | | | | |
| Discretion over when to take breaks from work | | | | | |

checklist for comparing alternatives

have to be translated into specific design objectives. Alternative proposals can then be evaluated against these objectives.

The design of work systems is normally carried out by a project team comprising the various disciplines needed to develop appropriate solutions. This team in many cases will include either those to be directly involved in carrying out the work or their representatives. Since members of the team are likely to hold differing views about the nature of employees the first step requires agreement about the specific design objectives relating to the needs of these employees. One approach to examining these differences of opinion is illustrated in Exhibit 25. This simple questionnaire can be used to examine differences of opinion among the project team and then, by sharing the information, discussion can lead to acceptance of a model of human behaviour to form the basis for the work system design. Often the views expressed initially differ widely as illustrated. The data presented was collected from a group of managers and specialists responsible for designing a work system. The next stage involves completion of a second questionnaire (Exhibit 26). The purpose of this questionnaire is to establish the goals to be achieved in the particular situation when designing jobs and work groups. Again wide divergence of view is to be anticipated initially. In comparing views expressed in response to both questionnaires inconsistencies may be found, e.g. E in Exhibit 25 and B in Exhibit 26.

Having agreed the goals to be achieved it is now possible for the project group to compare technical options more effectively in terms of human aspects. A checklist as shown in Exhibit 27 can be used to assess the appropriateness of the design of jobs and work-group activities and equipment and layout. Individual jobs can be assessed independently. Where the focus of attention is the work group, the second part of the checklist is applicable. Within this work group individual jobs may be left unspecified by the design team, these decisions being left to the work-group members themselves. It is possible, however, to use the first part of the checklist as a means of assessing the presence of opportunities for individuals to develop satisfactory jobs within the work group's tasks.

Comparison of feasible jobs in terms of the principles is now possible. Reference to the earlier part of the analysis will enable the preferred alternative to be identified. Clearly other factors also have to be considered when deciding which of the alternative designs to adopt. As stressed earlier, the overall objective is to match the organisational needs and those of the individual. Other factors will include an economic appraisal as well as consideration of the implications of the alternatives within the wider organisational context. Here we advocate the simultaneous consideration of these factors and the development of solutions providing the 'best fit' achievable.

The steps in the design process are summarised in Exhibit 28. As in the

112

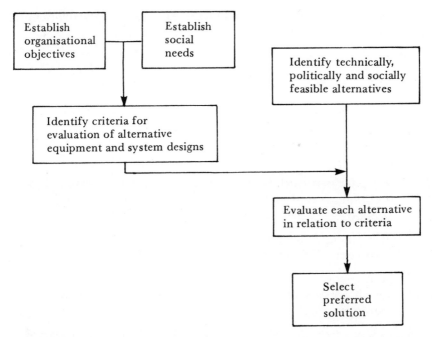

**EXHIBIT 28** A summary of an integrated approach to the design of new work systems

case of the steps in the process of planned change shown in Exhibit 18, the design process is unlikely to follow such neatly defined steps. The whole process is iterative. It is likely that the statement both organisational objectives and social needs will be clarified and elaborated many times during the design process. An examination of equipment capabilities may lead to a revision of organisational objectives. However, consideration of the approaches and use of the aids described in this section can result in a more effective integration of technical, operational and social needs in the decision about new work systems.

## SUMMARY POINTS

1    Seven stages in the change process were identified:

Awareness of need
Establishing goals
Diagnosis
Planning
Preparation
Implementation
Monitoring and evaluation

2   Different goals will be sought from the change by the different interest groups. Agreement is needed about 'how', 'when' and 'what'.

3   In diagnosing problems, aim to establish whether or not to proceed with change and then how to proceed.

4   Select from amongst the alternative structures for planning change that which allows for the preferred level of involvement for the interested parties, line management, staff and end user.

5   Preparatory work such as staff recruitment, selection and training, as well as management and end-user briefing are an important element in the change programme.

6   Incremental implementation is often attractive but the problems likely to result need to be considered.

7   Experience gained from a change programme if disseminated in the organisation can result in the avoidance of earlier mistakes.

8   Incorporation into the technical design process of consideration of the human aspects will result in less remedial change following installation.

# CHAPTER 8

# *The future of office work*

The development of new office technology and its availability far outstretches its current application in most offices. Up to this point we have been concerned to examine the implementation of technologies in the office which are already available. We have looked at some case examples of the implementation of changes in the office which be believe reflect the way in which new technology is introduced. We have drawn on the experiences of managers with responsibility for office functions in order to identify problems and assess the benefits resulting from those corrective actions taken. This resulted in suggested approaches to both systems design and change implementation. We will now look at the longer-term future of office work.

Recently the rate of development of new office equipment has been so great that it is difficult to appreciate that the microprocessor, the basis of much of this progress, was invented as recently as 1971. Any attempt to predict future developments is obviously speculative. However, here we are more interested in the rate of adoption of new equipment rather than the rate at which new equipment is developed. We shall attempt to identify some of the influences upon the development of the office and office work, and consider some of the consequences.

We will consider five themes in relation to the direction and pace of technological change; the development of the technology, and economic, political, social and organisational factors. Clearly these factors interrelate to influence the rate of technological change in the office.

## Technological factors

The idea of a fully electronic office no longer seems to be just a dream. In Chapter 1 we represented the functions of the office as the spokes of a wheel with the centre as the fully integrated and automated office system. Advances in the technology on each spoke make it feasible to automate many of these functions already.

Integration of the various functions is clearly an important step in the move towards the fully electronic office. At present manufacturers of equipment tend to be specialists operating in specific markets, i.e. telecommunications, computers and traditional office equipment. Even where manufacturers supply more than one of these markets, their organisations are usually divisionalised, based on product market. Consequently, in the past they have not been set up to supply all the needs of the electronic office from any one division. It is clear that at the present time there is little attempt being made to achieve compatibility between the equipment of different manufacturers. Some exceptions exist, but in most cases compatibility is not being sought even between equipment serving similar purposes and certainly not between the various types of equipment needed for the fully electronic office. This incompatibility of equipment acts to slow down the rate of adoption and change.

Developments in telecommunications will certainly lead to the increased linkage of equipment based at different locations. There will also be a considerable increase in the availability of public and subscriber information networks. An example in the UK is TOPIC. This is an information system developed by the London Stock Exchange for use by stockbrokers and others. This facility is available over the telephone for subscribers who can use a common television receiver for this service as well as PRESTEL, the Post Office's information service. This type of system is likely to be developed ocnsiderably over the next few years so as to give large numbers of users, both business and private, ready access to information on a wide range of topics.

The steadily falling cost of equipment will lead to much greater availability both at work and at home. As equipment becomes increasingly sophisticated, it will also become easier to use. It seems likely that most managers and many office staff will soon have ready access to terminals. Eventually, this access will not be confined to the office. The size and cheapness, as well as the ease of communications with other systems, will facilitate use at home. Problems of commuting to work may also lead to the home being used increasingly as an office.

Within the next ten years it seems highly likely that voice input to computers will be commonplace. Whilst it is possible already to 'talk to' computers, the facility requires considerable computing capacity. Improved technology and falling costs could lead to widespread adoption. Manufacturers are already developing personal vocabulary cards on which could be recorded the individual's voice patterns. Such cards would be used as a 'key' and, along with voice-recognition techniques, would enable computers to translate spoken language into operating instructions or text. The paperless office then becomes a reality since text originators and receivers by means of simple verbal commands could directly control information creation, dissemination, manipulation and retrieval.

Equipment will, in general, become smaller in size, lighter, quieter in operation, more versatile and more reliable. The output will also be of improved quality.

## Economic factors

The new office technology appears to offer many economic advantages to organisations: greater productivity, improved quality, more useful information and reduced overheads. However, capital investment in the office has, traditionally, been limited. Estimates in 1977 of the investment per office worker in the USA varied from $2000 to $6000, compared with an average investment of $25,000 per industrial worker. There are indications that this situation is changing. Growth in commercial organisations in the service sector and increasing competition, often on an international basis, had led to a reappraisal of investment policy for the office. Financial institutions, insurance companies and other similar large organisations are automating operations, often in order to speed up the services offered. Another study carried out in 1976 by an American research institute predicted that there would be considerable increases in investment in the office in order to slow down the increases in the relative costs of office and industrial employees. Equipment manufacturers predict considerable expansion in the market, e.g. in Western Europe a total market in 1976 of £55 million for word processors and £61 million for dictating machines is expected to rise by 1985 to £335 and £102 million, respectively. As large organisations automate office functions, others will follow, possibly in order to remain competitive but also in order to increase the efficiency of interorganisation communication.

Rising salary costs relative to equipment costs are certainly one factor influencing management decisions to invest in equipment. However, shortages of suitably qualified personnel, fears of increased staff militancy and the perceived impact of employment legislation will act as further stimulants to change.

## Political aspects

The rate of technological change will be influenced by political decisions. The policies adopted by central government relating to intervention in the development of new technology, intervention in encouraging its adoption and its role as a large equipment purchaser will influence the rate of change. The response of business organisations and trade unions will also be an important factor. Here we will focus upon the actions being taken by central government and trade unions.

Governments in most major countries throughout the world have formulated policies regarding the development of microtechnology and its applications (often described as information technology or informatics). In both the USA and Japan the state has offered practical encouragement. The European Economic Community is attempting to co-ordinate progress in its member countries in order to create both a pool of expertise and a strong home market for products. Elsewhere, for example in China, advanced technology is accorded high priority. The industrially less-developed nations are also seeking a share, often in the manufacture of components.

In the UK, central government funds have been allocated to encourage the adoption of microelectronic applications. The Micro-Industry Support Programme (MISP) and the Micro-Application Project (MAP) have been established for this purpose. Support for the creation of the manufacture of microelectronics components has been made available to new companies such as INMOS and NEXOS.

The policies adopted by different UK governments have varied but much of the onus for the development seems to have been placed upon commercial enterprises themselves. This contrasts with the emphasis in many other countries. As mentioned earlier, the French Government is encouraging widespread adoption and acceptance of new technologies by providing VDUs and computerised directories to all telephone subscribers. This, in turn, is likely to stimulate demand for further applications.

Generally, throughout the world, governments are supporting the development of information technology. This level of interest should lead to agreements being formulated covering such matters as communication networks across international boundaries and hopefully international standards.

Considerable interest is also being shown by the trade union movement in many countries. Earlier we referred to the work of the International Federation of Commercial, Clerical and Technical Emplyees (FIET). Their action plan is intended to help co-ordinate the response of its affiliated unions to problems of new technology both in the industrialised and developing countries. They advocate that governments take on a major responsibility for preventing technological unemployment. They suggest that unions take a positive role in encouraging governments to influence the actions of employers in regard to the interests of their employees. Facilities are sought for unions to be involved in decisions about new technologies.

In the UK, office employees have traditionally been less well organised than manual workers. Often staff belong to in-company staff associations rather than trade unions. However, as new office technology is introduced one would expect increases in the membership of trade unions. This in turn will probably lead to more active staff involvement in the processes of implementation. The FIET action programme identifies 'an urgent need for trade unions to become involved in the process of systems design'. As a direct result, one would expect that office managers and their advisors will be involved increasingly in discussions and negotiations with organisations representing their staff. Also one would expect increasing union membership amongst management whose jobs are likely to be affected by the changes.

## Social factors

Widespread adoption of new office technology will undoubtedly lead to reduction in the total manual workload. Whilst the new technology will result in new jobs being created, e.g. communications specialists and service engineers, it will also lead to the disappearance of many others in their present form. Political decisions will be needed to resolve these problems. These decisions are likely to have a profound effect upon working lives and the quality of life generally. A shorter working week, job sharing, early retirement and longer periods of education including sabbaticals are all seen as possible means for reducing the level of unemployment. It seems likely that most of us will have increased leisure time. The extent to which people see work as central to their life may change as a result of the increased emphasis upon non-work activities. Views about what constitutes work may well also have to change.

One opportunity offered by the new technology is for work to be dispersed. As indicated earlier, it will be technically possible for staff to be based at home and communicate with colleagues using teleprocessing systems. This could offer cost savings to employers but could also result in the kind of exploitation which has been a problem with other types of home workers, who have often been outside the normal employment legislation. The level of social contact might also make it a less attractive proposition to staff. An alternative approach would be for community workshops to be established (sometimes called neighbourhood workshops in the USA). They could be set up in or near residential areas. Equipped with a range of technological devices, they could be rented for the required number of hours by staff who would each be working for different employers. Control and security aspects would need careful consideration, but this type of centre could be cost-effective for employers and attractive to employees.

As office technology develops some skills will become redundant and staff will need to acquire new ones. Initially, most people are anxious about change and reluctant to accept it. Staff will need careful guidance. It is likely, however, that the ongoing acquisition of new skills and even the necessity to change career will become a normal part of modern working life. These changes will affect managers and professionals as much as, if not more than, junior staff in the office and may lead to the development of new career paths and strategies.

## Organisational factors

As indicated earlier there is an interrelationship between the themes of this chapter. Certainly, many of the problems encountered at the organisational level are political in nature. Accessible technologies have had an influence on the design of organisations. For example, many services are already often centralised, e.g. computing, mail and telephones. Others are often decentralised, e.g. secretarial support. The implementation of integrated systems in the office will cut across traditional job and departmental boundaries. Resources will have to be reallocated and organisation structures modified. Such changes inevitably will meet with resistance and some staff will suffer as a result of the changes.

Progress is likely to be impeded also by a lack of knowledge about the tasks, procedures and practices in offices. Systems often have been developed or evolved over a considerable period of time. Even when procedure manuals exist, they often do not fully describe the system in practice. In such situations, identification of equipment needs, selection of equipment and implementation will be slow and the likelihood of a speedy transfer to fully integrated systems in the near future will be lower. The design of integrated offices will require a combination of expertise from several existing specialisms, e.g. systems designers, O&M specialists and communications specialists. A shortage of the necessary expertise may well lead to a slower adoption of changes necessary for the fully integrated office.

The new technology is not only capable of undertaking productive work but also can be used as a means for increasing management control. As an example, word processors often have a facility for monitoring utilisation. Where such systems are interlinked, the supervisor may be able to call up any screen and observe the work as it is carried out. Additionally, records of daily performance can be made readily available. At a higher level in the organisation, rapid access to information can enable senior managers to monitor the performance of their subordinates. This ease of access to information gives the opportunity for greater centralisation in many organisations. Alternatively, the new technology could be employed in a way which gives more responsibility and control to those performing the tasks. Decisions will have to be made about the form of future organisations.

## SUMMARY POINTS

1   The pace and direction of future developments in the office are unpredictable. What is clear is that most of the technology required for the fully electronic office already exists.

2   Technological, economic, political, social and organisational factors will influence the rate of movement in the direction of the automated office.

3   Governments, business and trade unions will influence the rate of change.

4   The new office technology will lead to a reduction in the total work available. Strategies will have to be developed to cope with the potential problems of technological unemployment.

5   The shape and structure of organisations is likely to be changed to accommodate new integrated sytems.

6   The new office technology could be implemented in a way which permits staff greater freedom at work (hours, location) and offers jobs with more challenge and responsibility. Alternatively, the new technology could be used to deskill many jobs and exercise greater degrees of management control.

# Case studies

## Introduction

The case information included in the following case studies was the result of a project sponsored by the UK Petroleum Industry Training Board and the Work Research Group, the Administrative Staff College, Henley. During the two years of the project the authors worked with managers from the UK Petroleum Industry in introducing changes in the technology employed and the organisational structures and job designs adopted.

The cases were carried out in widely differing circumstances. Companies ranged in size from one hundred employees to many thousands. Some cases were in city-centre office blocks, others in offices at refineries and distribution centres. The companies included a small localised distributor, several subsidiary companies and major multinationals with control in the UK as well as Europe and the USA. The numbers involved in the cases also ranged from five to twenty-five and included staff in various functional departments: accounts, secretarial services, telephone sales, marketing administration, reprographics and general administrative services. The cases are, therefore, reasonably representative of the way in which clerical work is being undertaken in the UK and the changes in technology currently being introduced. The strategies for introducing change adopted here will certainly be used in introducing new technology in organisations in both the private and public sector.

Reference to Chapter 5, and Exhibits 14 and 15, in particular, will enable readers to identify those aspects of the cases which relate most to their own situations, whether in terms of background or problems being tackled. In each case description we have related to the steps in the process of planned changes described in Chapter 6 (see Exhibit 18). This has been included to demonstrate the stages in practice and something of the iterative nature of the process.

The material presented was collected from the twelve managers directly involved in the project as well as their colleagues and staff. Data were collected by the authors principally by interview, but the participants were asked to keep diaries of events occurring during the period of the investigation. The projects were evaluated in terms relevant to the organisations involved and the personnel concerned. In no case is there reference to detailed measures of productivity. It was assumed that improvement in aspects such as customer service, reduced unpaid overtime and smoother office functioning would also result in improvement from an efficiency point of view as well as for the people involved. The cases, whilst prepared by the authors, have been discussed with those directly involved.

*Introducing computerised systems in an accounts-receivable section*

| | |
|---|---|
| *Company:* | Computing and accounting centre |
| *Department:* | Accounts-receivable |
| *Staff:* | 15 (male and female) including supervisor |
| *Change:* | Introduction of VDUs for direct access to computer |

### Background

The department involved in this case was part of a subsidiary of a major oil company which had responsibility for data services for the parent company and its associates. In total, this autonomous company employed about 200 staff. The offices were situated in the South-East of London. Within the department the section involved in the project had responsibility for maintaining the accounts-receivable ledgers for the parent oil company.

The section was managed by a supervisor who had a team of two section leaders and twelve clerks (senior clerks and cash clerks). The section was organised into two groups, i.e. trade ledgers and specialist/manual ledgers. Cash clerks traditionally had sorted in-company payments and prepared them for entry to ledgers. Senior clerks had responsibility for maintaining ledgers, ensuring payments were correctly posted to customer ledgers and dealing with queries regarding accounts. The qualification board of the accountancy professions accepted the work as suitable for training future members of the institutions.

### Initial computer applications

When extending the mainframe computer applications into the accounts-receivable section the decision was made by senior management to operate both the manual system and the computerised system in parallel. Ledgers were to be updated on a monthly basis within the department. At the same time information about payments received was to be punched onto cards in a separate department and customer accounts updated. Clerks in the accounts-receivable section were to have access to customer files by means of VDUs in order to sort out any customer queries as they occurred. The separate credit control department required information about customer accounts on a daily basis and, in order to meet this requirement, the accounts-receivable section had to pass details of cash received for punching by mid-day.

The initial stage in the introduction of the system resulted in VDUs being introduced into the accounts-receivable section for the operation of the Master Record Programmes. About six months later an interrogation system was put on-line which enabled clerks either to look up the account if the customer's account number was known, or secondly, to search for the customer's account number, if not known. A facility for printing customer statements was also made available at this stage.

*Awareness of problems*

The staff had little difficulty in learning how to use the available programmes. However, even though they recognised the potential for the computerisation of accounting systems they experienced certain frustrating problems. The response rate of the system was found to be considerably slower and more variable than they had been led to expect. The use of printed ledgers would often have been quicker than the computer system. The systems designers had been assigned to new projects and appeared reluctant to spend time ironing out problems seen as either rather minor to them or an in-built failing of equipment. The computing department was located on the floor below the accounts-receivable section and consequently links between staff were limited.

Following the introduction of the computer-based systems the requirement to update accounts daily had meant that the accounts-receivable section had to process the receipts by mid-day. This necessitated a reorganisation of the work. In addition to the more junior clerks, the seniors were having to work at this task in the morning. The job of sorting incoming cash had now to be shared amongst all grades. When straightforward, this work, if shared, took an hour per day to complete. Queries resulting from difficulties in reconciling invoices had to be resolved as quickly as possible. These were dealt with by phone, but sometimes by correspondence. Generally, such queries resulted from either missing or inaccurate information from the client when paying. Whilst the company used a standard form when submitting invoices many clients would use the format of their own accountancy system for payment. In such circumstances clerks had to relate this information to their own company's invoice.

The section was organised to give each senior clerk responsibility for a section of the total list of accounts. These seniors were given basic guidelines for the work but had scope for using their own discretion in deciding the detail. The two section leaders were both located with their sub-section in an open-plan office with the supervisor positioned at one end, facing the other staff. When absenteeism or holidays occurred staff were required to cover, therefore, it was considered essential that staff had sufficient skill to enable this flexibility.

## Problem diagnosis

The next stage of computerisation would lead to the direct input into the systems via VDUs of information on cash payment and immediate debitting of customer accounts. The task of inputting the data was planned to be carried out by senior clerks, thus eliminating the need for cash clerks (all part-time staff). Prior to this change several problems in motivating senior clerks were either already apparent or anticipated:

1   Many of the senior clerks were pursuing accountancy qualifications. They tended to express restlessness and the feeling that the work available was not sufficiently demanding. Incorporation of the cash input tasks into their job was likely to aggravate these feelings. Apart from those times when changes to operating systems were being introduced the normal work routine would remain similar.
2   The cash input work being incorporated into the job of the senior clerk would probably lead to a lowering of job grade on the job evaluation scheme. Whilst not affecting the current salary of job holders it may create increased interest amongst individuals in moving to 'better' jobs.
3   The trainee accountants were mostly males. Their average stay in the department had tended to be two years. Young women, generally, were not found to be interested in obtaining professional qualifications. Whilst their average length of service was four to five years, they were usually slower to learn the work and less motivated to learn tasks

outside their immediate job. There were promotion prospects within the department and opportunities also existed elsewhere in the company. As these tended to be on the supervisory/senior side, opportunities were limited for movement unless staff sought such responsibility.

4   Systems designers and programmers in the past had not developed totally appropriate systems and staff using the system have had to 'muddle through'. Staff generally were expected to be adaptable in overcoming system inadequacies but these problems could be a source of considerable frustration to those staff operating the system. New systems had invariably been behind schedule and this itself caused problems with additional workloads over prolonged periods.

5   The credit department which was located next to accounts-receivable was a department perceived to have higher status. This was a source of unrest for staff in accounts-receivable.

6   The company for many years had been seeking means for manpower reduction. Over the previous five years numbers working in accounts-receivable had been cut by seven. Further computerisation was expected to lead to further reductions and these changes were interpreted by staff as 'more work and less people'.

The normal entry requirement to the job was five GCE 'O' level passes but those wishing to become qualified accountants required two 'A' level passes. At one stage approximately 90 per cent of the staff were female but, as pointed out earlier, the supervisor held the view that females were less flexible and that they were believed to 'panic at responsibility'. It had therefore, been policy more recently to attempt a 50/50 balance between males and females.

It had not been company policy to offer day-release opportunities to trainee accountants. A system of flexible working hours was in operation. Cover had to be provided up to 1640 in the afternoon. Senior clerks were sometimes required to work overtime. If this exceeded ten hours per month the senior clerk was required to obtain the supervisor's approval, otherwise he had discretion. Flexitime appeared to have reduced the amount of overtime worked. There was no trade union representing white-collar employees. Whilst there was no formal consultative machinery, other opportunities existed for staff to meet together. The office accommodation was recently completed. There was a shared management and staff dining facility and an active social club. There was also a personnel department available to deal with staff problems where appropriate.

The senior clerks were organised by the section leaders who were responsible for ensuring that the cash was completed on time, for checking that work was completed and for ensuring adequate cover for answering queries outside 'core' flexitime. They reported to the section supervisor who was involved particularly in work guidance and training. Additionally, the section supervisor was responsible for any disciplinary action.

## Planning change

During the course of the workshop several steps were identified for action to reduce 'motivational problems' amongst staff. Two specific objectives were stated: first to help employees adapt to new forms of work and secondly to help stimulate and retain interest. The changes proposed were:

1   Allocate specific projects to ledger assistants (senior clerks) designed to improve operational efficiency and assist with the implementation of changes to the systems. On completion project reports were to be discussed by the supervisor, the section leader and the individual concerned.
2   Trials with new system: consider behavioural implications; generate ideas about 'best way of working'; assessment involving management and those who have worked it.

## Implementing changes and their evaluation

During the six months following the workshop, projects were assigned to staff. The section supervisor reported varying degrees of success in stimulating interest but a contribution was made towards the implementation of changed sytems. Examples of specific projects were:

1   Investigation of errors in unallocated error listings — this project had remained incomplete because the senior clerk responsible had been promoted to a post in another department.
2   Setting up a procedure for recording queries on ledger cards with VDU implementation in mind — the senior clerk developed a new routine which was agreed by all staff. This senior clerk had later left the company after several unsuccessful attempts to gain promotion internally.
3   Setting up alpha keys for accounts-receivable. The clerk completed the task but reported that he found it boring. The task was repetitive, requiring the clerk to input standard information into VDUs.

4   Nudge listing design. This project was carried out by a senior clerk who required some assistance from the section supervisor. She needed 'chasing up' to ensure that the work was progressing.

Project work was seen by the section supervisor to have certain possibilities as an approach for stimulating interest and developing knowledge and experience. He reported that the males responded more positively, probably because of greater career orientation. Difficulties were experienced in a department with fairly routine work in identifying suitable tasks for projects. It may be necessary, in future, to look outside the immediate department for projects. Additionally, manning levels have been reduced to the point where there is little 'slack' in the system to allow staff free time for project work.

Whilst the new system for cash input had been delayed, six months after the workshop senior clerks were involved in cash input work. Whilst initially they did not welcome the work it became accepted. The task involved about an hour each per day. Following immediate implementation of the new system, the section leader had expected to have a revised deadline for the work, i.e. evening instead of mid-day. This had not been agreed at this stage but was seen as likely to remove some of the pressure on the senior clerks, who had only one VDU on which to input cash received.

One section leader had recently gained promotion and as a result a senior clerk had been promoted to section leader. A senior clerk had left the company having failed to gain promotion on three occasions. As a result of discussion about matching the needs of individuals and jobs offered, the new posts had been advertised without indication of career opportunities in accountancy. Those appointed during the six months following the workshop had been less career-orientated than many previous staff and appeared to have settled down better into the routine of the department.

Other changes introduced involved staff correcting their own errors. Previously all error correction was carried out by one clerk. This clerk still processed errors but now had to find out who made the error and pass the information on to the clerk concerned for correction. Whilst the clerk who previously corrected all errors believed it quicker to correct the mistake herself, the section leader reported that the other clerks as a result had knowledge of where they were making errors. One of the control clerks had been involved in ledger work, having been made responsible for a small section of ledgers, i.e. covering Southern Ireland. No job regrading was possible in the short-term but he had been promised a visit to Dublin on business as compensation. Also the experience was seen as beneficial from a career viewpoint.

It was the intention in future to operate a job-exchange system. At any one time two clerks would exchange jobs for a one-month period. The section leader was enthusiastic and staff had responded well to the idea. Difficulties existed in implementation primarily because of the training time required. When there was turnover of staff in the department, insufficient 'slack' existed to permit more than one person to be trained at any one time and exchanges had to be suspended. In the supervisor's view considerable advantages were to be gained from having staff familiar with all the jobs in the section.

*Later outcomes*

At a workshop 13 months after the initial workshop the supervisor reported that the mix of staff (25 per cent seeking qualifications and promotion, 75 per cent prepared to plod along) was more satisfactory. The office had become more settled, a low standard of work was no longer a problem, nor did staff appear to find the work as boring. The supervisor also found himself able to give more individual assistance to the 25 per cent seeking qualifications. The atmosphere was happier, with less 'agitation'. There was no staff turnover during the six months before the second workshop compared with 50 per cent per annum, previously.

The new VDU system was introduced behind schedule, eleven months following the initial workshop. Section leaders and staff had been regularly consulted with regard to the changes. Whilst premature to make evaluation the staff appeared to have adapted well, although considerable time was spent in training.

---

**DISCUSSION POINTS**

1  Recruitment policies should be reviewed regularly, particularly when changing technology is having an impact upon the skills required.

2  The user's expectations about the benefits of computerisation are often not met.

3  Changes in computer-based systems are usually introduced in stages.

4   During implementation, operating dual systems can put stress and strains on the staff for periods beyond those initially anticipated.

5   Customers are unlikely to be prepared to modify their own systems to fit in with those of suppliers.

6   Adding job interest by means of project work will only be satisfactory where sufficient system slack exists for staff to complete the task to their satisfaction.

7   Inadequacies in systems design are often compensated for by staff operating the system. This can be a source of frustration.

8   Previous experience of change will influence attitudes towards further planned changes, e.g. 'more work and less people'.

CASE STUDY 2

*Developing a strategy to cope with likely changes in a small final-accounts section*

---

*Company:*    Trading subsidiary of an oil company

*Department:*    Final-accounts section

*Staff:*    6 (male and female) including section leader

*Change:*    Work procedures associated with computerisation

---

*Background*

The department involved in this case was responsible for the accounts within the main trading subsidiary of a major oil company. The accounts department in total employed approximately 200. In the two years prior to the project much of the work performed had become more highly computerised. This had resulted in considerable changes in work roles. Whilst there had been no redundancies, some of the staff had been transferred either as a result of the changed manning levels or inability to cope with certain changes. The section concerned here dealt exclusively with the final accounts (quarterly and annually). The section leader had five subordinates. In addition to supervisory duties, the section leader had certain specific duties including all VAT returns. These were duties that had proven difficult in the past to delegate. The deputy had also had certain specialist duties in addition to general supervision. Three clerical assistants performed general clerical duties including the control and reconciliation of accounts and the production of schedules. A fourth clerical assistant maintained the master code list. This job was likely to be changed radically as a result of the increased computerisation. There was a peak in workload towards the end of each quarterly accounts period.

## Problem awareness and diagnosis

The final-accounts section had experienced changes in procedures in the previous two years and further changes were anticipated. A major reallocation of duties had occurred during the period at approximately six-monthly intervals. Individuals normally experienced difficulties in coping with such changes. Usually the section head was not in a position to influence decisions about change. Staff were normally 'consulted' about detailed implementation of such decisions but not the major decision itself prior to it being made. Training on the job was available and, where possible, work was arranged so as to create a dependency between the clerks.

Much of the work carried out by the clerks was self-regulated. They could decide the extent of 'policing' undertaken on ledgers in order to explain slight discrepancies. Where queries arose the auditors might have requested an explanation in which case the clerk responsible would have been required to investigate unless able to give an explanation. Awareness of discrepancies and prior policing helped clerks to respond to auditor's queries more immediately.

In a situation where accuracy in detail was essential, the section leader considered it imperative that staff demonstrated a sense of responsibility. In order to achieve this he organised the work so that there were defined boundaries to the responsibilities held by each. It was the management's policy in the department to move staff around the unit. Within the section the work was rotated between those clerks with similar duties. Normally, when absenteeism occurred the other team members coped with the increased individual workload, an aspect thought to indicate a high team spirit. The tasks were allocated in such a way so as not to create competition between individuals but rather to foster co-operation.

## Planning change

Certain changes in computerised systems that would affect jobs performed were identified during the course of the initial workshop. An action plan was drawn up with the objective of coping with the changes anticipated in the following procedures:

1   Segment accounts and reports.
2   Evolvement of asset acquisition programme.
3   Accounting of leases.
4   Automatic production of published accounts.
5   Possible transfer of master code list to another department.

6   Take-over of accounts — stocks of plant/equipment and platinum.

The following steps were identified as the means for implementing the changes:

a   Consult specialists in order to establish nature and extent of changes
b   Assess likely effect of changes on the section — tasks, work-load, organisation and staff
c   Hold a meeting of all staff to plan in detail implementation of changes
d   Gain management approval
e   Publish the plan
f   Finalise training schedules for all staff
g   Issue a working timetable/checklist for staff taking account of all changes.

## Preparing for changes

Following discussions with specialists a staff meeting was held at which the reallocation of workloads commenced. Preliminary decisions about staff training needs were also made. The staff's preferred reorganisation of the work was not possible without changes to the existing rules about access to confidential data. Senior management later endorsed this change. A detailed plan reallocating the work was agreed and published.

A management working party, including the section leader, was set up to detail changes to the master code list. This working party, meeting twice weekly, was to report back to senior management at six-weekly intervals. The section leader consciously involved the current job holder in discussions about changes and she attended several meetings of the working party.

## Implementing changes and their evaluation

During the six months between the workshop and the first review of progress many of the changes had been implemented. A comparison between the automatic production of accounts and the former method showed very favourable results. The systems department had sent a congratualatory note to the section leader regarding this aspect.

Many minor 'bugs' still existed in the system, however, and the task of rectifying these required the experience and knowledge of the section leader. Regular meetings had been held in the section to discuss the state of affairs, establish objectives for the next period and develop detailed plans. Problems were experienced during the changeover in coping with the workload, particularly in processing leases. Outside assistance was sought but even so the work was not carried out to the normal standards.

Additional difficulties throughout the period resulted because a staff vacancy had not been filled for most of the time. The first person offered a job, internally, had had an accident which resulted in a prolonged absence. A second person had filled the vacancy but this had meant additional training being required in the section above that needed to prepare for the changes in procedures. Not all changes were introduced during the period.

### Further problem diagnosis

Immediately following the deadline for the quarterly accounts (five months into the study), management detected a lowering of staff morale. This caused concern because of the normally high morale in the section, especially since a recent re-evaluation of jobs had resulted in upgrading for staff, except the section leader. There had been a noticeable increase in the outspokenness of staff and the extent of 'disgruntled' comment. One clerk had recently failed her Institute Examinations. Additionally, she was unenthusiastic about recently assigned duties which were seen by the section leader as offering opportunities for self-development, e.g. evolvement of the asset acquisition programme. Uncertainty also surrounded the job of the clerk responsible for the master code list.

### Corrective action

The section leader did not think that the problem resulted from influences in the company outside the immediate section, high technical demands, pay or job design. Rather, possible causes were identified as:

1 Frustration resulting from the extent of changes being introduced.
2 Annoyance at anomolies in the job evaluation exercise.
3 Perceptions of low promotion prospects.
4 A lack of goal and achievement feedback.

### Further change implementation

Steps to be taken to investigate and resolve the problems were:

1 Discussion with staff to identify and agree problems leading

to low morale (work and non-work). Individual and group meetings to be held with the section leader.

2   To ask staff for suggestions on means to resolve problems.
3   A monthly reporting vehicle from staff to management.

*Awareness of future problems*

This approach to tackling problems is likely to be the one adopted by the section leader in the future as further changes are introduced. It was envisaged that during the next three to five years the section would experience an increase in automation which would eliminate much of the routine work. It seemed likely that staff would tend increasingly to fall into two groups. One group would consist of managers and technicians responsible for interpreting data, problem-solving and progressing the work, the other carrying out administrative work which had not been written into the automatic procedures probably because of the cost involved. Also when system changes were being introduced staff would be needed to operate a manual system during an interim phase. It was anticipated that automation would probably lead to a slight reduction in staff numbers.

In the future, staff in the section will probably be required to show more flair and imagination as well as be willing to develop knowledge and skills in system design. Project work will be employed as a means for assisting staff develop their skills as new technologies are introduced. Those responsible for implementing change are likely to have to overcome problems of low motivation and a lack of enthusiasm for change. Higher management will have to consider staff attitudes and hold regular discussions with staff to enable views to be exchanged openly and frankly.

---

### DISCUSSION POINTS

1   Staff involvement in decisions about the organisation of work can lead to benefits for both the manager and staff.

2   Staff shortges during periods of change and uncertainties about the change are likely to increase the pressure and lead to reduced staff morale.

3   Technological change in accounting offices is likely in the short term to increase the division of work into professional and machine operation. In the longer term, data input into the system may be automatic.

137

CASE STUDY 3

*Low staff morale in a small general accounting department*

---

*Company:*　　Multinational oil company

*Department:*　General accounts

*Staff:*　　　7 (male and female) including chief accountant

*Change:*　　Reallocating tasks to improve job interest and increase motivation

---

*Background*

The department involved in this case was responsible for the accounting function of the exploration divison of a major overseas multinational oil company. The company's UK office, situated in central London, employed about 70 personnel involved in managerial, administrative and technical work. The division was responsible for organising exploration and development of North Sea Gas reserves but was not itself an operating division. The department processed financial information for management, handled all financial transactions with suppliers, contractors and its one customer (British Gas) and prepared final accounts. In the twelve months immediately prior to the project as many as eleven separate accounts had been completed dealing with different contracts with outside organisations for major exploration or development activity. The division had responsibility to an overseas head office which imposed particular demands upon the accounting department and then also its own set systems.

The pressure of work in the department was closely related to the level of activities in the North Sea. Just prior to the study the total workforce in the department had expanded considerably with increased workload. Nevertheless, this workload varied quite considerably. As many as 2000 invoices may have been handled in any month and up to 500 suppliers dealt with.

Clearly, new work depended upon the discovery of new reserves as well as the company securing involvement in exploration. The department manager considered that people in the industry recognised the uncertainties and were not noticeably affected in their everyday lives.

The department consisted of seven people, organised as shown in Exhibit A. The chief accountant had overall responsibility for financial and cost accounting as well as data processing for the division. The financial accountant was professionally qualified with two to three years experience but a recent appointment. The analytical accountant, also at that time a recent appointment, had not yet qualified. The computer operator/programmer, whilst based in the accounts department, worked throughout the division. Two of the clerks were female and one male. One of the females was 19 years old and in a recent staff appraisal had revealed herself as unclear about her own work aspirations. The other female was middle-aged and familiar with the work, having spent several years in the department. The third clerk was in his mid-twenties and had only been with the company for a short period prior to moving back to Australia.

Turning to personnel policies, it had been the normal practice to employ temporary staff from agencies to cope with increasing workload unless the trend was seen to be long term. The manager believed staff to be comparatively well paid with a salary differential of approximately 70 per cent between junior and experienced clerks. Additional to the basic salary there was a half-yearly bonus, daily luncheon vouchers and loans for travel

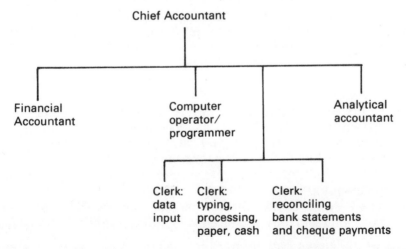

**Exhibit A**  Organisation of accounts department (as described by the chief accountant)

contracts. The social and sports club had developed considerably over a twelve-month period and was well supported by young members of the staff. Clerks were expected to have a 'searching brain', good interpersonal skills and to 'fit' into the division, in addition to possessing the normal clerical skills. Staff were not generally members of trade unions.

A system of flexible working hours had been attempted in the division. Personnel were allowed to choose their time of arrival (0900, 0915, or 0930) and then leave at quarter-hour intervals from 1700. There was no clocking-in system and it was thought that any changes would be resisted. The system had been abused, some staff tended to arrive late but still leave early and the arrangement had then been withdrawn. Management also experienced difficulties in co-ordinating activities and providing necessary cover when flexitime was in operation.

*Problem awareness and diagnosis*

At the outset of the study the manager identified several aspects of the job which appeared to be contributing to a lower level of staff motivation than desired, i.e.:

1 Difficulty in developing interest amongst clerks when the work was largely repetitive. They did not appear to appreciate their role in the overall operation and they saw little in the way of 'end product' from their efforts.
2 Inability of inexperienced staff used to manual systems to understand complex output from the computer.
3 Difficulty maintaining interest amongst younger staff once trained to do the work.
4 The lack of promotion prospects for relatively highly paid clerks either internally or in other companies and their acceptance of the position.
5 Perceived status and pay differences between clerks in this department and secretaries elsewhere in the office. The secretaries were bilingual and highly skilled and they received higher compensation as a result. Their workload normally afforded them more time to relax and talk to their colleagues.
6 The systems to be operated had been designed in the parent company and they appeared very bureaucratic to all involved.

One of the clerks had been given the opportunity to learn about computer input work.

## Change planning

Following the commencement of the study the manager decided to reallocate the tasks between the clerks in order to make work more interesting for all of them. He also planned to observe which tasks suited each clerk and attempt to develop their skills to match the demands of the job. Additionally, jobs such as data input to the computer were to be available to the clerks to give them an opportunity to learn new skills and develop new expertise. The manager considered he was not in a position to change either systems or job gradings.

## Change implementation and evaluation

Six months later a procedure for staff appraisals had been instigated. This had given the manager the opportunity to explore aspirations and feelings about current jobs and his staff's expectations of the company.

During the early part of the study the complexity of the work had reduced due to lower levels of company activity. The level of paperwork had been reduced by 50 per cent and more work had been computerised. To some extent the spare capacity had been used in developing two further computer applications.

## Changing events play their part

The most senior clerk during the period experienced personal problems which had to some extent distracted her during work time and resulted in her delegating work to the other two clerks. This had produced positive results from the point of view of the overall department. The tasks had been reallocated and each clerk learnt a wider range of tasks than in previous jobs. There was overlap of skills and increased flexibility amongst the clerks. This added interest and enabled clerks to appreciate and understand departmental operations to a greater extent. Another change resulted in clerks having to make contact with staff in other departments. This also added interest and developed their understanding of the wider organisation and interrelationships as well as the relevance of their own tasks. The clerks had started to deal with most of the queries from suppliers without recourse to the chief accountant. The financial accountant who had developed knowledge of the departmental operations would probably be appointed to a newly created position of deputy chief accountant with responsibility for analytical accounting and clerical functions. This would create a career opportunity which was not available in the earlier departmental structure. One clerk would be trained to input data to the computer when time was available for her to attend a suitable course. The secretaries with whom clerks tended to compare themselves had more recently appeared to have had more even work-loads and therefore differences seemed less apparent.

Turning to the future, changes are likely to result in more sophisticated applications of the computer. This was thought likely to improve management information but not likely to have an immediate impact on the clerical jobs.

---

### DISCUSSION POINTS

1   The design of the work organisation must take into consideration the variability of the work-load which may be affected by factors far removed from the manager's influence, e.g. oil discoveries, government policies on taxation and world-wide oil prices. In this case work-load was variable and increases unpredictable.

2   It is often difficult for employees to see how their work relates to the wider needs of the organisation. This is likely to be further exacerbated if systems are complex and data collated remote from decision-making.

3   If the manager has a clear view of his own aims and objectives an opportunist approach to implementing change can be adopted.

4   Often skills and abilities remain untapped and greater flexibility in work organisation can create opportunities for their use.

CASE STUDY 4

*Group working in a general accounting department*

| | |
|---|---|
| *Company:* | Multinational oil company |
| *Department:* | General accounts |
| *Staff:* | 11 (male and female) including senior accountant |
| *Change:* | Job content redesigned as a result of computerised systems |

*Background*

This case, within a US-based multinational organisation, involved a department that was responsible for general accounting. The UK organisation refined, distributed and marketed petroleum products. The accounts department was responsible for the control of capital and revenue payables. Within the department, finance and general accounting services were provided for the manufacturing and marketing operations. Also, administrative control activities were carried out which resulted in the determination of the net trading results and balance sheets for the UK company. Procedures adopted had to comply with requirements specified by the US Head Office.

The senior accountant in this case had concern for a section of the department with ten subordinates whose task was to examine company trading payments and capital expenditure to ensure that proper authority for payment existed in accordance with company procedures for approving payments; expenses were properly charged to company accounts; payments were in accordance with terms agreed with the suppliers and met all exchange control, taxation and statutory requirements. The section was also responsible for administrative control over company capital appropriation and projects, fixed assets and the preparation of regular management reports. Occasionally special studies also had to be carried out, e.g. feasibility studies for new capital projects.

The staff of five male and five female clerks included two post-qualified accountants who were responsibile for financial reports, fixed-asset accounting and meetings with project managers. A senior clerk was responsible for all payments. Three clerks checked invoices against purchase orders, as well as ensuring additional certificates were presented, e.g. UK construction industry tax deduction scheme. Each clerk was responsible for specific aspects of the operation, e.g. refinery, transport, construction. All invoices were checked and batched for computer input. When payment had been made, all invoices were filed. (Four clerks batched invoices and carried out filing duties, a job normally performed only by juniors for three months when first appointed.)

All new employees were required to have attained GCE passes at 'O' level and some would have been more highly qualified. The better qualified may have sought training to become members of the Institute of Chartered Accounts.

## Problem awareness and diagnosis

The senior accountant expressed the view that much of the work, since it only involved checking invoices, was repetitive and boring for staff. He found difficulty in maintaining the interest and hence commitment of the more junior staff. At the time, two of the junior clerks were less than 20 years old, one about 25 and one about 40.

During the first workshop several action points were proposed with the objective of increasing the motivation of the junior staff, i.e.:

1  Increasing the responsibilities of the staff checking invoices by involving them to a greater extent in problem-solving.
2  Arranging for occasional visits by staff to those locations with which they had dealings.
3  Reallocating work in order to increase the variety available in each job.

## Change planning and preparation

On return to the department the senior accountant held a meeting with all his staff at which he discussed the general plan and possibilities available for change, as he saw them. Staff appeared enthusiastic and agreed to proceed.

It was decided by the staff at a group meeting that work should be subdivided on an alphabetical basis. A programme was set up to train all clerks to carry out all the tasks involved in the total process in order that each sub-group could handle a section of the alphabet. Seniors within each sub-group were made responsible for training the clerks in the new skills required.

## Change implementation and evaluation

The changes were implemented and operating within a two-week period. Time was available within sub-groups for staff to undertake special projects. On the whole, the changes were implemented fairly smoothly, the exception being one of the older staff who had difficulty adapting. Although initially enthusiastic, she experienced problems fitting into the new system and it was eventually decided that she should be given one task of her own rather than being required to work on all tasks within a sub-group. This was accommodated satisfactorily within the overall departmental operation.

## Further change

Major organisational changes were announced shortly after the workshop. This ultimately resulted in the complete transfer of staff from this section elsewhere in the department. Also the section manager was made responsible to a new manager. A new deputy and third-in-charge were introduced into the section. In having to cope with an influx of new staff it was decided to revert to the old system and teach each new clerk one skill at a time. When staff had acquired the skills essential for one job it was planned to revert to a multiskill approach and reorganise into sub-groups, since this was believed to benefit the organisation because of increased job interest and commitment as well as greater flexibility amongst staff. A period of three to four months was believed necessary for staff to develop the basic knowledge and skills and to settle down in the section before reorganisation was feasible.

## Further diagnosis

Further reflection following the workshop led the manager to question recruitment policy. The manager believed that the mix of age and skills may be inappropriate for the tasks required. This aspect was to be considered more fully.

Morale, however, was believed to be high in the department. When projects had to be completed within a tight deadline, staff were willing to work overtime, some without additional pay. The junior jobs appeared to attract young people who viewed them as a first step in a career. For these younger people the traditional organisation offered them only very routine work but in some cases this was seen as appropriate by the manager since it gave them an opportunity to learn about the organisation. The sub-group system, when eventually implemented here, was seen as the likely model for work organisation in other sections within the department.

---

## DISCUSSION POINTS

1   Division of the total work by client groupings rather than task specialisation can create more demanding work for individuals.

2   Group working where the group has clearly defined responsibilities and where each individual can perform all the tasks within the group's responsibility can improve job interest as well as increase organisational effectiveness.

3   Some individuals will prefer working independently to working in a team. It is usually possible to organise work in a department in a way that will accommodate some individual working as well as group working.

---

CASE STUDY 5

*Staff consultation over changes in a*
*sales accounting department*

| | |
|---|---|
| *Company:* | Multinational oil company |
| *Department:* | Sales input (part of accounting) |
| *Staff:* | 9 (male and female) including supervisor |
| *Change:* | Involvement in problem-solving and decision-making and in changes related to increasing computerisation |

### Background

This case concerned a major oil company employing approximately 120 staff in its sales accounting department. This function was divided into sections of varying sizes according to the work performed (see Exhibit B).

### Sales input

The section in question dealt with sales input from locations geographically spread around the country, not all of which were controlled by the company. Input arrived as either hard copy through the ordinary mail or in coded format over data transmission lines. The information flow is shown in Exhibit C.

The section employed one supervisor (male), eight clerks (three males and five females). Most of the staff were aged below 25 years, but the range continued to 40+. Length of company service tended to be long with the supervisor having served over 20 years. Only two staff had less than three years' service (see Exhibit D for details).

In outline, tasks were:

1    The opening and sorting of mail.
2    Completion of input controls records.

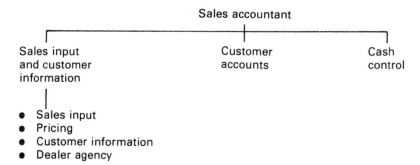

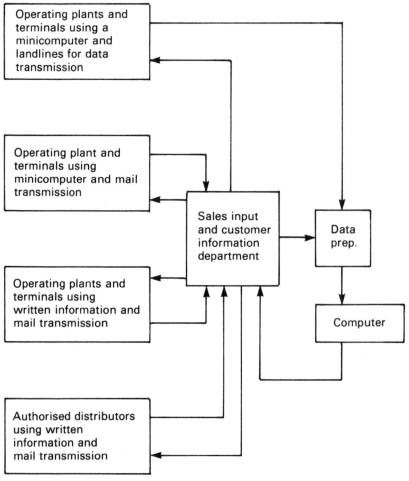

**Exhibit B**   Sales accounting: organisation chart

**Exhibit C**   Sales input: information flow between the department and both the company operating plants and terminals and authorised distributors

| Age | No. of staff | Sex | No. of staff | Length of service | No. of staff |
|-----|-----|-----|-----|-----|-----|
| Under 25 | 5 | Male | 4 | Less than 5 years | 4 |
| 26-30 | 1 | Female | 5 | 5-10 years | 4 |
| 31-40 | 2 | | | 10-20 years | — |
| Over 40 | 1 | | | Over 20 years | 1 |

**Exhibit D** Staff structure in the sales input and customer information department

3 The control of documents to and from the data preparation department.
4 The receipt of computer output.
5 Dealing with queries from the computer runs and from document originators.

The processed documents were returned to the sales input section and customer information prior to transfer to a central filing unit.

*Problem awareness*

The work was seen as repetitive and sometimes pressured, with high volumes to be handled within defined time limits. Increasing use of the computer had tended to make certain aspects of the work remote from the section and consequently staff had reduced opportunities to develop an appreciation of the total accounting system.

*Problem identification*

The problem identified in the section by the sales accountant was essentially lack of team spirit. In his view staff seemed to show little interest in activities outside their immediate work area. They seemed to want to avoid responsibility and were unwilling to become involved in problem-solving. He aimed to improve performance by using whatever available opportunities existed to increase interest in the work.

Before attending the workshop a number of possible approaches were considered:

a Encouraging the supervisor to delegate more work.
b Persuading the supervisor to give wider job training to clerks.
c Establishing ways of giving clerks an awareness of the results of their work.

149

*d*   Improving the variety of tasks present in each individual's total job package.

*e*   Trying to eliminate routine elements of the job.

Whilst these were not necessarily alternatives, some means would be more difficult to implement since they involved people outside the immediate section, the department and in some cases the company.

At the workshop it emerged that considerable effort would probably be necessary to involve the supervisor in bringing about change as he had been in the post for a number of years and was considered to be fairly traditional and rigid in his approach.

With increases in the extent of computerisation, it had been planned that more input would be received over data transmission lines, but directly into the sales input and customer information department. For this purpose a minicomputer had been installed in the section. It had been planned to appoint one clerk as machine operator but at the workshop it was suggested that this provided an opportunity for increasing job interest for all clerks.

## *Change planning*

A number of points were formed into an action plan at the workshop:

1   Increase the variety of the individual clerk's work by extending the clerks' duties to include problem-solving related to their tasks.
2   Increase variety in clerical jobs by training clerks to deal with those operations associated with use of minicomputers.
3   Improve the understanding both of their tasks and interrelationships by arranging for clerks to visit outside plants and by organising training sessions with other areas in sales accounting.
4   Measure existing workloads to determine equitability between clerks (subsequently dropped as there were no complaints about inequity).
5   Introduce a daily progress report for completion by clerks in order that a system of performance measurement can be introduced.
6   Produce job descriptions for each member of the section and define group objectives.

## Further change planning

In the month following the workshop, the manager organised a staff meeting away from the work situation. It was conducted in an open session where staff were invited to contribute ideas on ways of improving the work organisation, i.e. it was hoped that staff would suggest solutions to problems. This resulted in a number of actions:

1. Staff suggested improvements to the document storage system which saved time and resulted in greater security. Implementation involved consultation by the manager with managers outside his department but agreement on change was reached and subsequently came into operation six months after the meeting.
2. Staff suggested that documents, properly completed, should be mailed already sorted into numerical sequence, thus giving an added check to sender and receiver and avoiding a frustrating task in verifying omissions. This involved people outside the department and company, revealed training needs, and could not be implemented immediately. It was left for the manager's attention at a later date.
3. Staff suggested that they would be better able to adjust their working pattern if they had early notice of the need to reallocate tasks. This related particularly to providing job cover for absentees. It was agreed that the supervisor would look for early help in preference to taking a directing role towards the end of the day.
4. Operation of the minicomputer. The use of this machine was discussed and it was agreed that the senior clerk would be trained in its use and that she would then be responsible for training other members of the group so that it could be operated on a rota basis. Not all members of this section were enthusiastic about using the machine, but agreed to the training.
5. Means of increasing the clerks' knowledge and awareness of their role and their level of responsibility were discussed. As a result the clerks asked to use their own name in all correspondence with the people outside the department (rather than acting under the signature of the supervisor as in the past). The manager agreed to write to all remote locations to give them the name of the clerk responsible for handling the receipt of documents for that location. It was also agreed that clerks would visit their 'locations'.

## Change implementation and evaluation

Interviews conducted with the manager, supervisor and clerks some four months after the workshop showed a number of different reactions to the changes. The manager was generally pleased with the more co-operative and responsible attitude of his staff. Some had already visited other locations and plans were in hand to extend this. However, the cost had restricted the opportunity for visits between clerks and the most distant locations. Clerks were handling more queries and all of them had by that time received training in the use of the minicomputer.

The supervisor was still handling a large number of queries and continued to need encouragement to delegate. He had been given some additional tasks by the manager in order to encourage him to release some of the more routine elements to be handled by the clerks. He still tended to regard as inexperienced and often preferred to handle the clerks enquiries himself rather than give the necessary explanation to the clerk. Some of the clerks, in practice, found the responsiblity for dealing with queries a worrying challenge and were inclined to seek help from the supervisor. This seemed to be mainly a factor of experience and confidence.

Some clerks were unclear about the objective of the staff meeting at which changes had been initially discussed and thought it was to provide information for the manager. One said that he felt it very difficult to be objective about a job which he had done for many years. Generally, however, clerks appeared to be pleased with the greater contact they now had with the remote locations and particularly with their accountability for correspondence.

It was anticipated that further meetings with staff would be held to encourage their suggestions and involvement in the wider sphere of operations. Even with this limited result, the improvement in team spirit was thought to have been sufficiently marked from the manager's point of view for him to extend the approach to other groups within the department when suitable opportunities arose.

## DISCUSSION POINTS

1   Staff can contribute effectively when involved in problem-solving activity.

2   Consultation over change can result in a view of problems differing from that held by the manager. The changes proposed in such circumstances are also likely to be different.

3   The consultative process for planning change needs to be set up carefully in order that those involved recognise and understand the objectives.

4   A change in the managerial style of the supervisor is often the key to improving jobs from the staff's point of view.

5   Individuals are likely to need advice and support for sometime after being assigned new responsibilities.

6   Technological change often creates new tasks and demands new skills. A rethink of work organisation can lead to more job interest for staff generally or it can lead to the employment of one or more specialist staff.

*Technological and work organisation changes with unanticipated outcomes in a marketing administration department*

| | |
|---|---|
| *Company:* | Oil products marketing company |
| *Department* | Marketing administration |
| *Staff:* | 23 (predominantly female) including manager |
| *Change:* | (1) Improvements to increase motivation; (2) Identification of task-training needs associated with the introduction of VDUs |

### Background

The company involved in this case dealt mainly with the marketing and distribution of lubricants and associated motor products. The particular department involved in the study was concerned with marketing administration and was divided into two sections, one dealing with invoicing and the other with credit matters. Both sections reported to the marketing administration manager who in turn reported to the marketing director.

Work in the department involved the receipt and processing of delivery documents in connection with the sale of the company's products. These documents formed the basis of computer input. Invoices were prepared by the computer. The department also dealt with queries and certain aspects of credit administration. A substantial portion of the work of the department was essentially routine, e.g. checking and collating documents, and batching them for computer input.

Staff in the department totalled 23, including the manager and two supervisors. The manager was male and there was one male junior, the rest being women covering the complete working age span from 16 to 59. Some staff had achieved considerable knowledge of the products as well as company procedures and were able to identify errors on input documents and take corrective action. They liaised with the originators of the documents and with customers concerning queries.

## Problem awareness and diagnosis

The manager identified two major problems in his department: motivation and a change in the method of work operation. Whilst the problems cannot be separated in practice, they are described separately here. Detailed analysis revealed that the second problem had more far-reaching effect than the former.

*Motivation*　Motivation in the department was seen by the manager as critical. The manager described his staff as generally co-operative but not interested in the work. Salary levels compared well with other employers in the area. This tended to lead to low staff turnover but some staff did leave, mostly it seemed due to family reasons.

Management and staff had been holding meetings to discuss the problems and future plans. Usually these meetings resulted in an immediate improvement in productivity but this diminished over the period of the few weeks between meetings. At that stage the manager described his objective in holding these meetings as being to achieve motivation without the 'big stick approach' and to develop an openness between staff and management. The meetings seemed to the manager to lead to the motivational cycles.

*Working method*　For the smooth running of the department staff needed a sound job knowledge concerning the company's products, pricing policy and procedures. Nevertheless the skills needed were basic manual ones — batching, collating, etc. However, it was planned to link the department directly to the computer by means of visual display units (VDUs). This would involve some reduction in staff numbers and those remaining would have to learn new skills such as keyboard operation and would have to accept the screen instead of paper as the input medium.

## Change planning and implementation

VDUs had already been introduced in other parts of the company and the manager was aware of reported adverse effects on staff in terms of morale and the different training needs. Some staff, particularly the older ones, were anxious about new equipment and the manager was concerned that his staff should be

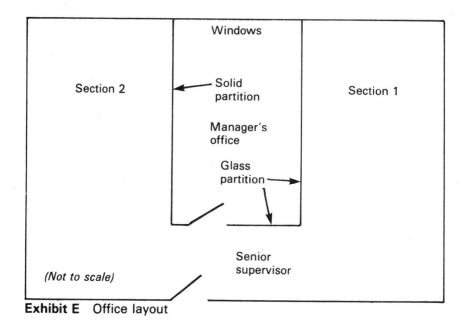

**Exhibit E** Office layout

introduced to VDUs in a way that was non-threatening and that the opportunity should be taken to increase job interest.

Following the workshop he planned to involve the staff in designing the new jobs associated with the equipment. His aim was to ensure that staff continually had interesting and meaningful work. He believed that this would be achieved by training so that all staff could perform all functions carried out by the department: VDU operation, clerical work, customer queries and credit administration.

Some VDUs were subsequently installed with no real problems at the time. Two employees started to wear spectacles for the first time shortly after this but there was no conclusive evidence that this was directly attributable to the use of the VDUs and the medical department were kept informed.

In the workshop session the manager developed an action plan to have separate meetings with both sections and to ask them to analyse the situation and suggest their own solutions. In the event these meetings did not take place. Instead one of the supervisors made discreet enquiries and it emerged that part of the problem concerned competitive and discriminatory feelings between the two sections (see Exhibit E) and the fact that in work crisis staff from Section 1 were asked to help Section 1 but not *vice versa.*

Although the physical arrangements could not be substantially changed, practical efforts to improve the situation resulted in staff being regularly moved between the two groups to help with work peaks in both sections. In addition, the manager and the two supervisors continually emphasised the need for co-operative working and the importance of all staff in the department.

An interview with the manager and one of the supervisors some six months after the workshop suggested this particular problem had been solved.

### Further change planning

At this stage the finance department became concerned that individuals were handling too much of the accounting process with consequent possible lack of audit control. They questioned the rationale behind the division in accounting responsibilities between the marketing and finance departments. It should be remembered that marketing accepted responsibility for marketing administration but the finance was responsible for data control and credit control, i.e. marketing had responsibility for all accounting activities not within the scope of the finance function.

The finance department reviewed the organisation's accounting procedures and recommended the integration of all accounting functions and demonstrated that the staff saving achieved by the use of VDUs in marketing administration could be increased by such organisation.

Moreover, it mitigated against the possibility of fraud since the work could be more easily controlled when organised conventionally within one department. The proposal resulted in an integration of the various departments with discreet division of work amongst employees. The previous marketing administration clerks became input clerks receiving delivery data and entering this through VDUs. Audit control argued that even when errors were evident these clerks must not be permitted to correct them.

### Evaluation

Six months later there was considerable dissatisfaction amongst staff and frustration at the reduction in job interest which job segmentation brought. Because of the more rigid divisions the employees were not able to use their existing job knowledge to take corrective action even when they could see this was necessary. There were no signs of an immediate resolution to the problems which were thought ultimately to lie in the eventual change to recruitment of staff more suited to the new work requirements.

This case shows the importance of anticipating and assessing all possible outcomes and consulting all parties when redesigning those apparently not directly involved. In this instance, the unusual circumstance of two major departments sharing responsibility for an accounting function contributed to the difficulties in implementing a change and finally resulted in less rather than more interesting work being offered staff.

---

### DISCUSSION POINTS

1   Working with new technology can offer new job challenge and hence interest. It may be possible to organise work so that all staff have the opportunity to develop new skills and knowledge.

2   The layout of offices and the arrangement of work-places can affect motivation in ways often not immediately recognised by management.

3   Established procedures and systems will limit the choice available for the design of jobs and work organisation. Conditions imposed by interested parties outside the work areas can dramatically affect the nature of work and job satisfaction of a group of staff.

4   In assessing the relative merits of alternative proposals for change at the workplace, consideration must be given to the impact on wider aspects of the organisation.

---

CASE STUDY 7

*Problems of introducing work processing into a large divisionalised organisation*

---

*Company:*     Multinational oil company

*Department:*  Communications (in the Head Office)

*Staff:*       8 (including 2 men) in administration service centre; 5 in word-processing centre (unit growing during period of study)

*Change:*      Introduction of word-processing systems

---

*Background*

The department on which this case report is based was part of the UK organisation of a multinational petroleum company. The department had a functional responsibility within head office for all aspects of communications, e.g. telephone and mailing services, secretarial and clerical work. The UK organisation was divided into divisions which each had a high degree of autonomy. The department co-ordinated communications between divisions and advised each division about methods for meeting its needs. The department was also responsible for assessing long-term needs and identifying technological developments likely to result in cost savings. The introduction of increasingly sophisticated equipment for processing communications was leading to a reassessment by executive management of the department's role within the organisation. Word-processing technologies, in particular, had been seen to demand a more co-ordinated approach to information processing if the staff savings required to justify the investment were to be achieved.

This case report is concerned with the implementation of changes following the decision to introduce word-processing systems. Prior to this, arrangements for secretarial facilities differed between divisions within the company. Some divisions, in addition to personal and shared secretaries, had central typing pools to undertake more routine work such as long reports as well as typing for junior managers. In some divisions no typing pool existed. In each case the division was responsible for deciding the level of clerical and typing support necessary, although assistance was available from the communications department concerning both O&M as well as appropriate techologies.

## Problem awareness

Early experience of word-processing systems was confined to systems with relatively sophisticated functions but limited to one keyboard. This experience led the communications manager to several conclusions. It was recognised that this equipment, whilst appropriate for specialist work, had limitations when considered for wider use. Firstly, much of the organisational work could have been performed on less sophisticated equipment, thus reducing capital outlay. Secondly, operators had difficulty transfering from conventional typewriters to the new equipment, partly because of unnecessary sophistication. It was also widely recognised that any new systems to be introduced in the head office had to be compatible with each other thus enabling transfer of information between systems as well as operators between divisions.

It was decided that a Logica-Unicon system be used for normal typing work. Each unit was to accommodate up to twelve terminals and there would be sharing of units between divisons. Each division would have its own central word-processing section with about three operators. Peaks in workload and lengthy documents would be processed in a separate section within the communications department. In this section there was to be a more sophisticated system. Also this section would eventually have more personnel than others. New employees would be trained within this section. When absenteeism occurred in one of the divisions this section would provide replacements. Any temporary staff employed would work in the central unit, where supervision would be higher and the work more suited to temporary staff.

For centralisation of typing facilities in the way described to be economic, it was considered necessary that secretaries formerly dispersed throughout the division be relocated to a central location and the work reorganised. An examination of the work of the secretaries had led to the conclusion that the typewriter was in use for only a small proportion of the total working day (between 15 and 25 per cent). Other duties included filing, arranging meetings and visits, taking dictation, etc. Following centralisation this administrative work was to be provided within administrative service units alongside the word-processing sections. The telephone system had the facility for dictation to central offices.

Following early experience it became company policy to implement word processing anywhere in the organisation where clear savings could be shown to result. It was estimated that a reduction in total secretarial support of 60 per cent was necessary if savings were to be achieved from the proposed system. This assumed no increase in workload resulting from the changes, e.g. managers deciding that more information should be typed rather than handwritten, or verbally communicated. In these estimates an assumption was also being made that a machine utilisation level of approximately 70 per cent would be achieved.

In order that the service level afforded users remained similar or improved (but with the reduction in staff required), the personnel involved would have to operate much differently than previously. It was expected that operators would need to be at their workplace continuously during longer periods. Managers would have to share facilities and priority rules would need to be established. Operators, instead of being directly responsible to one or several managers, would be managed by a supervisor. Direct contact with the user would be exclusively over the phone since users and operators would no longer be in close proximity and shorthand would then be replaced by audiotyping. The user would also have to develop telephone dictating skills.

Since a high degree of autonomy existed in each division the divisional management would decide the extent to which word processing and administrative service units would replace personal and shared secretaries. They would also determine the rate at which change would be introduced.

*Problem diagnosis*

The communications manager was confronted with several problems:

1 How should the word processing and administrative service units be organised in order to be economic and achieve acceptable service levels for users whilst also meeting the needs of those employed in each section?
2 How should changes be introduced?
3 What role is appropriate for the communications department in managing these systems?
4 How should an integrated communications system utilising available technologies, including word processing, be designed?

161

### Change planning

The strategy decided upon for introducing change was to start with one word processor in the communications department. Having gained experience, implementation to other sections and divisions would follow. The first unit, located in the communications department, would serve two sections. Following this phase in implementation, user surveys in other divisions would be the basis for establishing the equipment and personnel requirements in each division.

### Implementation of change and evaluation

In the event, the first unit installed was actually operational in an existing typing pool prior to its operation in the communications department. This typing pool employed mainly mid-career women with several years' service. A supervisor was responsible for organising the work and ensuring the maintenance of an appropriate level of customer service. She was accountable to a senior supervisor who was also responsible for administrative services including local mailing and telex output.

No reorganisation of the department resulted from the introduction of word processing. VDUs replaced typewriters, one printer served four VDUs and the processor was remote from this section being located several floors below.

In contrast the second section operational was in the communications department. Here no typing pool existed. Secretaries were reorganised into the central section. The new section was seen by the communications manager to offer an opportunity for reappraisal of the method of organisation and the design of jobs. He thought that the more traditional form of organisation in traditional typing pools offered less attractive jobs than those formerly held by the junior secretaries. In addition to the possiblity of a reduction in status he anticipated that job evaluation would result in a lower grading for the new jobs than that of the junior secretaries. Also the variety present in operating the equipment was thought to be lower than present in the junior secretary's work. Promotion and career prospects would also probably be perceived as reduced.

The manager decided to allow the staff, through consultation with their supervisor, to determine their own organisation. The opportunity was created for an integrated word processing and administrative service unit. If staff desired to carry out all the tasks they could do so. The unit was located in refurbished offices, the result of a major modernisation programme. Staff were involved in deciding the layout. Following the discussion with the manager the staff decided that they would prefer to rotate between all the tasks in the office, rotating on a weekly basis.

Implementation of the full system in the communications department was slower than planned due to delays in the building schedule and because a study to determine administrative work-loads was also delayed. The word-processing unit was set up in temporary accommodation. Several months after relocation staff were not carrying out administrative duties. Two reasons appeared to have caused this situation. Initially the unit was severely pressured to achieve typing output and lacked resources to undertake administrative work. Secondly, the study of work-loads had not been finally completed in that management acceptance was awaited. Management were not prepared to allocate further resources until the findings of this study had been agreed. The supervisor, however, was responsible for one clerk performing filing and general office services within a particular department. Other clerks working in specific departments would eventually be assigned to this supervisor and their base relocated to the central offices.

During the early stages following introduction there were several technical problems. The power supply fluctuated as a result of interference from the building works and problems were experienced with the software. The staff initially enjoyed the work associated with the word processors. They believed that the glamour would soon wear off and consequently wanted to develop a wider job role. Being the only word-processor unit in the office block the system attracted many visitors. One of the reasons for the visits was to introduce users to the system and help them appreciate its advantages and limitations. They were then thought likely to press for implementation in other divisions. However, resistance from managers in other divisions to the loss of personal or shared secretaries continued to be experienced. Criticisms made by users about service levels were felt by the communications manager to not be totally justified.

The supervisor in the communications department was also responsible for the running of this first word-processing unit. Before this appointment she acted as the communication manager's assistant. She had been involved in the word-processing project for a year before the system was introduced and also liaised with manufacturers regarding new software as it became available. She visited the manufacturers to inspect new software and organised visits by sales representatives to demontrate these developments to her own staff. Her job had been evaluated one level above word-processing operator — on a par with junior secretaries. If the job developed with the introduction of further systems she would be further upgraded.

The operators in the communications department allocated work amongst themselves. The supervisory role tended to have developed into that of systems specialist, adviser and trainer. This system of working and proposed method of organisation appealed generally to the staff in the communications department. They were all relatively young, several having been transferred from another office.

When temporary staff drawn from employment agencies were employed they would not normally be expecting to work with VDUs and a word-processing system. They would then often be concerned at the apparent complexity of the machines, and some would not stay. Once familiar with the equipment, however, the supervisor found that temporary staff began to be interested and committed to the work.

The staff in the other office with word-processing facilities were experiencing more difficulty in the changeover from typewriters to word processors. This resulted from personal problems as well as a less than ideal office layout. In this area, as in the communications department itself, two adjacent offices were used for word processing and administrative services. Unlike the other configuration where word processing and administrative services were in one office and printing in the other, in this area the word processing was located in one office with the administrative services in the other. The word-processing operators were in a relatively small office which also contained the printing facility. Consequently, noise levels were high, the span of vision of operators was restricted by the equipment and the office appeared cluttered.

For the start-up period of operation staff from the typing pool had all been redeployed on the word-processing equipment. Whilst the office served a group of approximately 80 staff, those staff who earlier had private or shared secretaries still had this service. Consequently, the word-processing unit was over-manned.

The supervisor in this area reported that her staff were generally satisfied with the new equipment once they had got used to it. One person, who was both deaf and dumb, had particular problems of adjustment. She had coped well with traditional copy typing, but was extremely nervous of the new equipment. Additionally she had reported eye-strain as a result of using the VDU, as had the supervisor.

The new equipment was operational, but at a relatively low level of efficiency. The supervisor had restricted her interest in the new equipment to that installed in the immediate work area. She seemed to view the VDUs as alternatives to typewriters and therefore her responsibility. On the other hand, the central word-processing unit was outside her office and therefore her sphere of responsibility. She was not enthusiastic about the new equipment, had shown no interest in gaining an understanding of the total system and resisted any shared responsibility for the central word-processor unit.

In contrast to the communications department's office, the extent of staff briefing and training was low. This reflected the level of interest of the two supervisors. The younger supervisor, from the communications department, had taken on the role of briefing both groups on new software. The communications department group had been exposed to more training from suppliers.

The extent to which users had been briefed on the new equipment and its capabilities also reflected the knowledge and enthusiasm of the two supervisors. At this stage the supervisor in the former typing pool believed that the workload had not changed overall but reported that the user was tending to request more changes to the text, often resulting from misapprehensions about equipment capabilities.

As pointed out earlier, the administrative services were organised from an office adjoining the word-processing office. In addition to a supervisor in overall charge of both offices, there were two male clerks. Both clerks were in mid-career and neither typed. Integration of the administrative and word-processing services would have been problematic in this area where staff were middle-aged and used to a more narrowly defined task.

## Dissemination of findings

Based on these experiences the communications manager made recommendations to senior management regarding the establishment of word processing and administrative service units to serve a department or division. He believed that the work organisation to be operated within his own department was to be preferred generally to the more traditional approach in the other department. Staff flexibility and willingness to rotate between tasks created the potential for lower overall manning levels. Each case, however, would have to be considered individually. Clearly in the other department circumstances limited the available opportunities, i.e. typing pool staff already established, male clerks unable to type, two separate offices, an existing typing pool supervisor, older staff. The final decisions about the organisation of these facilities were to be made by the local line management. It was hoped, however, that the communications department unit would become the model for other installations. It was planned to carry out all training in this unit prior to equipment installation. Working practices would then be transferred to other divisions. Whilst word-processing units were operational elsewhere in the UK in other parts of the organisation, they did not appear to be on the model proposed here. Consultations had taken place with managers from other locations with installations. In one case word processing had replaced typewriters in typing pools and the average length of service of staff in the sections was six months.

## Further problem awareness and diagnosis

Regarding wider implementation, it was seen as important to establish a successful first application. Much management resistance was seen as stemming from the relevance secretaries have to the manager's status. To overcome objections it was important that the communications department could demonstrate a similar level of user service at less cost as a result of the change to word processing. Cost savings also needed to be clearly established if the communications department was to demontrate the benefits of the centralised organisation of the administrative services and word processing. In such circumstances executive management would strongly support the changes and divisional management would have difficulty not adopting new technologies and working practices.

No major concern was expressed regarding staff redeployment or redundancy since a rapid turnover of staff existed and as new equipment was introduced the establishment would be gradually reduced by curtailing recruitment. Promotion prospects for junior secretaries, typists and clerks were very limited under the former arrangement since senior secretaries were normally appointed from outside. The senior job generally demanded working knowledge of foreign languages as well as other attributes and skills not normally found amongst junior secretaries. Supervisory jobs would still exist and opportunities to become expert in the management of new equipment and its installation would be created.

Within the communications department, one manager had specific responsibility for investigating the alternative communications systems and assessing their potential application. He had an assistant responsible for training personnel as word-processor operators, assisting in setting up new word-processing units and the development of these systems. This department, when recommending the word-processing system to be adopted, would do so with due consideration to the organisation's total communications needs in the context of the developing technologies. Commitment to one word-processing system had been considered with regard to the extent that it might limit future decisions to adopt technological advances.

The communications department was responsible for the equipment and its maintenance. Divisions using the system were charged as for other communications services, e.g. mailing. Staff, however, traditionally had been appointed by divisional management. Whilst the communications department believed maximum equipment utilisation would be achieved if staff were centrally controlled, such reorganisation appeared unacceptable to divisional management. The communications department believed that they should be responsible at least for the design of jobs and systems, specification of working methods, and provision and isntallation of equipment and training. Divisional management would then retain responsibility for employing staff, conditions of service, salary, disciplinary action and day-to-day management. A co-ordinating committee of section heads under the chairmanship of the communications manager was responsibile for ensuring a co-ordinated service between divisions.

## Further evaluation

No formal method had been established for monitoring and evaluating the changes and no historical data relating to performance were available for comparison. Records in the form of time-sheets and output were being kept but it was unclear how the volume of work had been affected by the changed technology. In the communications department the manager held regular informal meetings with the staff, 'drip sessions'. These meetings were intended to enable managers to identify and resolve problems at an early stage. Following a period of operation staff appraisals had been completed in this department. These indicated generally that staff found the work satisfactory. There had been requests by staff, however, for a specialist to carry out all printing duties. This was not seen by staff as an attractive job particularly since it was done in a separate room and in rather noisy conditions. The manager was resisting such a move since it was still planned, as had been agreed earlier with staff, to rotate staff through all the jobs.

# DISCUSSION POINTS

1   Technology offers an opportunity for the integration of information and communications systems. In large organisations communications experts will be needed to develop such systems.

2   If a specialist communications department is considered necessary, its role, whether advisory or operational, has to be decided.

3   Alternative work organisation arrangements can often be identified. No one approach will satisfy all the needs of the staff involved. Assessment of alternatives on narrow criteria can result in immediate operational goals being achieved at the expense of later costs, e.g. labour turnover and staff inflexibility.

4   Certain fundamental decisions regarding the eventual shape of communications systems have to be made centrally and at an early stage so that an incremental approach to implementation, if adopted, will result eventually in an integrated whole.

5   Managers as well as operators will have to accept new ways of working if the full benefits of word processing are to be achieved.

6   Participative approaches to designing work organisation within the limits of the total system design can be effective in achieving working arrangements more satisfying to the staff involved. Often these decisions will be taken late in the total decision-making process and the choice available limited by earlier decisions. However, usually such decisions have traditionally been taken at the local level and are probably better taken there if at all feasible.

7   Planning the implementation of new systems could benefit from a consideration of both optimistic and pessimistic forecasts of time involved.

8   Considerable training and support may be necessary to assist both operating staff and users to adjust to new technologies. Investment in training, for example, is often a very small proportion of the total investment but can have a considerable pay-off for the organisation as well as helping staff and users overcome their own fears.

# CASE STUDY 8

*Motivating staff in a reorganised reprographics department*

| | |
|---|---|
| *Company:* | Oil refinery |
| *Department:* | Reprographics |
| *Staff:* | 5 (male and female) including section head |
| *Change:* | Work reorganised to increase flexibility, to improve jobs and to increase motivation |

## Background

Changes in the reprographics department at a refinery formed the basis of this case study. The refinery was one of several in the UK operated by a multinational organisation. The department involved was responsible for the administration of forms used in the refinery (design and control), the printing of company forms, the microfilm service within the refinery and the control of copying throughout the refinery. In total the department serviced about 2000 employees at the location, 750 of whom were staff. A total of approximately 1900 different forms existed at the refinery.

The department supervisor had an assistant, two operators and one designer. A recent organisational change aimed at reducing staff numbers had resulted in one supervisor, grade 7, being appointed to manage both printing and design to replace two supervisors, grade 8. Two lithographic machine-operators, grade 9, had replaced three operators of similar grade. An assistant supervisor, grade 8, had been appointed. No change had been made to the job of forms designer, grade 10.

The supervisor was responsible for operating a forms control programme for the refinery and co-ordinating forms design with head office requirements. Also he was responsible for formulating the overall work plan for reprographic services for the refinery. Specialist advice was provided on technical aspects of reprography. A confidential film processing service was made available. A decentralised copying service had to be maintained.

Subordinates operated composing/drafting tables, lithographic machinery and copying equipment.

The tasks involved in operating lithographic equipment were mainly of a mechanical nature thus requiring mechanical aptitudes. One of the litho operators was 19 years old. The assistant supervisor was 24 years old. The second operator was older than the assistant supervisor, having been by-passed for promotion.

### Problem awareness and diagnosis

In this department the supervisor was concerned to discover means for motivating staff in the context of a refinery where staff numbers were being reduced. Additionally, bright staff were required to perform tasks which to them were seemingly without purpose. The one older operator, in particular, lacked motivation having been overlooked for promotion.

The company in the past had offered early retirement as a means of reducing staff numbers. Also clerical service units operated in the refinery and reprographics department staff, in previous reorganisations aimed at reducing numbers, had been offered training opportunities with the possibility of transfer.

### Change planning

At the first workshop the supervisor drew up an action plan with the aim of improving the motivation of the younger staff working in a skilled but restricted environment lacking in career opportunities. The following steps were proposed by the supervisor:

1  In order to increase opportunities for job rotation and work sharing upgrading to the form-designer's job to grade 9.
2  A rota system within the department so that staff do all types of work.
3  Involvement of operators in future equipment selection.
4  When future staff reductions occur, involvement of operators in administrative duties.
5  Further development of a day-release scheme to train staff for work in clerical service units.

### Preparing for change

The action plan was seen by the supervisor as a long-term plan. Whilst agreement could be reached almost immediately to involve operators in future equipment selection, however, no consideration of new equipment was imminent. The rewriting of the form-designer's job, management agreement and subsequent re-evaluation was seen as likely to require nine months, after which job rotation would have been feasible. Staff reductions were expected between two and three years following the workshop. Day-release programmes also required the approval of management.

## Change implementation and evaluation

Six months following the workshop the job of form designer had been redefined and a new job description produced. The supervisor's manager, having agreed in principle, was of the opinion that existing staff would not accept the change and so change was postponed. Recruitment of a replacement for the form-designer, however, gave an opportunity for the supervisor to introduce the idea of a multiskilled job. Additionally, an organisation and methods assistant left and these tasks had been incorporated into the work of the reprographics department. This additional work was thought to ensure re-evaluation of the form design job at grade 9. The form-designer referred to earlier had moved to the print room for training. No formal pattern of job rotation had been established at this stage, although staff were being involved in planning such a scheme.

Regarding involving operators in equipment selection, the supervisor indicated practical problems. The staff were seen as lacking the knowledge required if they were to influence equipment selection in any major way. The supervisor was to some extent responsible for this state of affairs. The staff reported that information about new equipment was not made readily available to them, nor apparently were they encouraged to develop the necessary knowledge. Following equipment selection, staff normally received on-site training from the equipment manufacturers.

Allocation of the tasks formerly carried out by the O&M assistant also appeared problematic. Much of the administrative work did not lend itself to distribution. The assistant supervisor had been made responsible for planning and scheduling work-loads and investigating machine problems, calling maintenance when necessary. It was proposed to change the procedure so that operators became responsible for contacting maintenance directly. The supervisor was concerned that the form-designer's job should not be seen by others as a junior supervisory position, therefore any administrative work re-allocated had to be distributed between form-designer and operators. The assistant supervisor, however, was unlikely to be promoted since the supervisor himself was unlikely to move or be moved and erosion of his duties could lead to discontent particularly in a situation where career opportunities were not apparent.

The manager preferred to employ female staff because normally they left the job after several years. As a result he felt they were less likely to get bored with the tasks. However, the work involved heavy lifting and consequently he felt at least one man was needed in the department.

The day-release programme enabling staff to experience clerical work extended over a six-month period. The longest serving reprographic operator who had worked in the department for seventeen years, had sought and been granted transfer to the reception area following a day-release programme. This appeared to have been highly satisfactory for all the parties involved. A second operator had then been placed on the day-release programme.

---

**DISCUSSION POINTS**

1  A lack of career opportunities will be a source of demotivation for some staff.

2  Job rotation can have advantages for staff, e.g. increased skills, interest and pay, and also for the employer, e.g. greater flexibility and increased efficiency. Disadvantages from a staff point of view include a devaluation of the individual's skills and for the employer, higher training costs and increased staff marketability.

3  Changes aimed at improving staff motivation may require the agreement of senior management. Even agreement to those changes which do not appear to affect other work areas may take considerable time. Changes to departmental establishment are likely to have wider organisational implications. The use of existing opportunities, e.g. day-release and staff transfer, may be more fruitful avenues to pursue.

4  Involvement of staff in decisions formerly made by the supervisor is not normally possible without changes in the attitudes and behaviour of the supervisor concerned.

5  In deciding to make changes the implications of alternatives must be as fully considered as possible.

---

*Group working for clerical services*

---

| | |
|---|---|
| *Company:* | Refinery |
| *Department:* | Administrative service units |
| *Staff:* | 30 (male and female) clerical staff |
| *Change:* | Group working for clerical services |

---

## Background

This case description concerned the development of clerical service units at a refinery in the UK. The refinery site was one of several in the UK organisation of a multinational company. For many years the organisation had been concerned about the level of manning at the refinery and many changes had been introduced since the early 1960s.

The early changes introduced in 1966 involved the creation of administrative service units (ASU) to replace the more fragmented clerical service. These units were set up with several aims including a reduction in staff, improvement in services, standardisation of clerical practices and procedures, increased opportunities for advancement through job enlargement and increased productivity resulting from improved morale and job satisfaction. Initially the ASUs were to cover activities such as mailing, filing, and copying and also the more routine clerical/administrative activities. Over several years the ASUs became responsible for considerably more complex tasks.

Following a 'management by objectives' exercise in 1960, it was considered that better co-ordination and control would result if the clerical and secretarial services were separated. As a result clerical service units were set up to cover administrative demands in five main administrative areas:

1  Technical recording/security/laboratory.
2  Accounting/plant operations/utilities.
3  Maintenance/construction/data administration.
4  Technical records.
5  Mailing/filing/copying/distribution systems.

The personnel in each clerical service unit were organised into groups based on a geographical split of the total work. Each group was responsible to a multiservice clerk capable of directing or carrying out any task required by the group. As an illustration of the arrangements, in the services and methods department four work-oriented groups with varying manning levels and multigroup leaders were responsible to the clerical supervisor. A futher four technical clerks reported directly to the supervisor. In all, thirty staff were involved, dispersed over thirteen refinery locations and organised into logical groups to meet customer needs. These groups provided clerical services to eighteen departments, mailing and general administrative work in six administration buildings, GPO and head office incoming and outgoing mail, receipt/processing/distribution, duplication/addressing/distribution of internal information and maintenance of refinery distribution list systems.

Each multiservice clerk was required to have a working knowledge of all tasks within his own group and at least three or more tasks in one other group. Each clerk was expected to assist in tasks falling within his team's sphere as well as some non-routine work or special projects as required. These clerks were expected to plan their own work routines, develop their own procedures and assist in determining the work standards required. Within groups there were both senior clerks and junior clerks.

The changes to the organisation can be seen from a comparison of Exhibits F and G. This new organisation was seen by management as offering viable career development prospects with opportunities for individuals to enrich their jobs. Clerks were recruited as school leavers and joined the clerical pool. On average they progressed to senior clerk within two and a half years and could later move on to become multiservice clerks. As a result of the changes considerable manpower savings had been achieved overall. The manager judged the arrangements as successful since staff appeared satisfied, sought promotion opportunities within the department and refused opportunities in other departments.

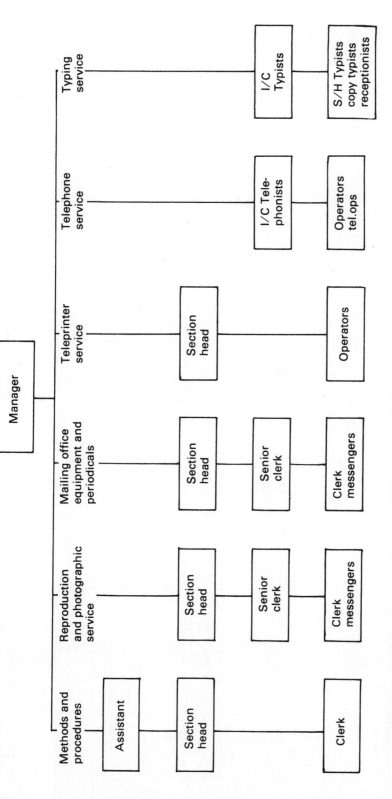

**Exhibit F** Organisation of office services and methods department in 1965

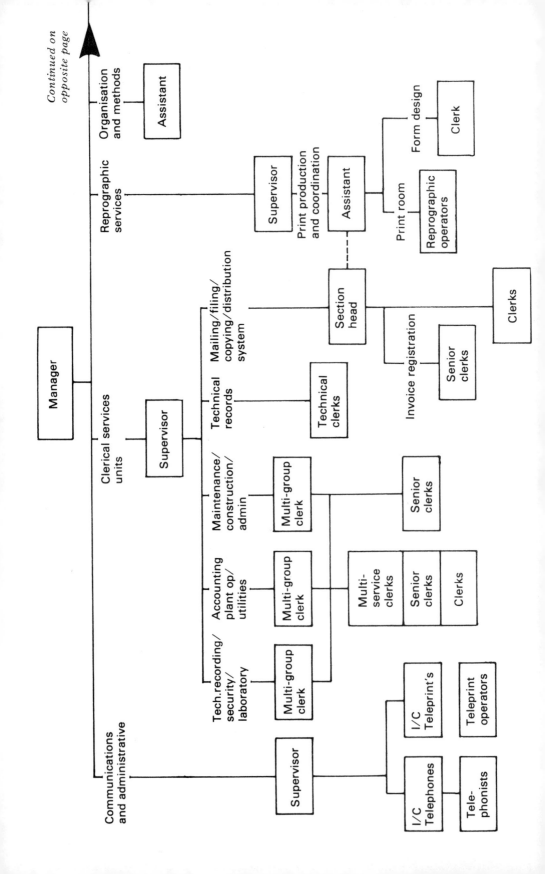

Continued on opposite page

Continued from opposite page

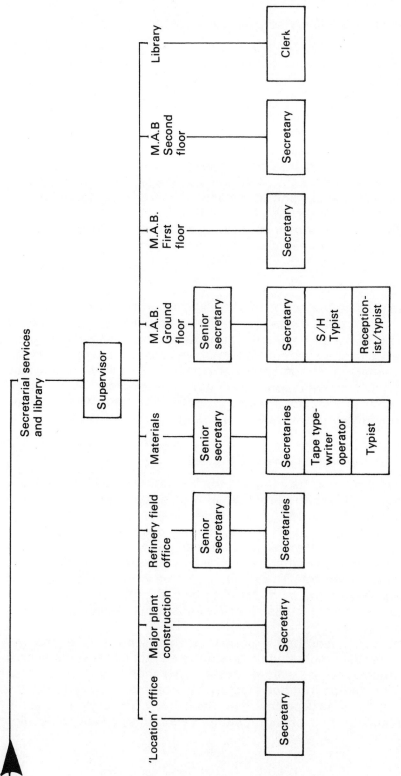

**Exhibit G** Revised organisation, 1977

### Problem awareness and diagnosis

Despite these opportunities offered, the supervisor of the clerical services unit reported at the workshop the following observations:

a    Young intelligent personnel became bored once they had been trained to carry out routine tasks and they were completely familiar with all aspects of the work. Difficulties were experienced in motivating these staff unless they were given frequent new challenges.

b    In an environment where the volume of refinery throughput was low and manning reductions were being sought it was difficult to motivate personnel.

c    Problems existed in motivating older workers (aged 45 to 60) who had limited potential for advancement.

### Change planning

During the course of the workshop several steps were identified in an action plan. It was felt that older employees could be more effectively used in training young staff. The younger and those more intelligent staff could be more involved in study groups with the managers of customer departments. A review of the jobs involving the staff concerned could be possible. Also scope appeared to exist for training personnel to meet the demands placed on them at work by the changing technologies.

### Change implementation and evaluation

A review six months following the workshop highlighted several changes. Initially the problem with older workers was to some extent resolving itself. Two older staff, one of whom was particularly difficult in the supervisor's opinion, were due to retire. The difficult employee had been given tasks away from the younger staff. The other person had made a useful contribution to training young staff. The remaining three workers over 50 years old appeared to be more satisfied with the job as it existed. The supervisor had concluded that it is important to select the right job for the person.

The supervisor had experienced that some of the younger workers resented being requested to do additional tasks even if this increased the variety present. He had found that these feelings had been influenced by the reception received from the managers in the department in which they worked. One manager, for example, had encouraged the accounting clerks to develop new ideas about working practices and they had responded well. The clerical service unit's supervisor also encouraged managers to suggest solutions to the problems relating to their department's clerical services, and suggest new working methods. The younger managers particularly had shown interest. One manager had arranged for clerks to visit control centres for appreciation training so that they could better understand their own roles. The supervisor reported that increasingly he was involved only in conflict situations and questions of resource allocation.

The supervisor was involving all his staff in the review of new equipment. It was now departmental policy to request potential suppliers to bring new equipment to the location either for trials or demonstration and staff were given the opportunity where possible to operate it. In addition he circulated staff with information and extracts from journals of those items of new equipment felt to be of interest. All the staff were to attend computer appreciation courses since much of the work would eventually become computerised.

---

### DISCUSSION POINTS

1   Clerical working practices should be regularly reviewed to ensure that in addition to meeting the needs of the user, the wider objectives of the organisation are being met as well as those of individual clerks.

2   In some circumstances group working can achieve considerable organisational gains when compared with rigid individual job descriptions.

3   The satisfaction and job status of older workers can be enhanced by making them responsible for aspects of training. Obviously such factors as personality and skills will affect the suitability of any one individual.

4   Technological change will affect the clerical function considerably. An appreciation of available new technologies and discussion about their applicability should reduce the uncertainties of individuals when changes are made.

5   Early and planned training in new ways of working will aid the implementation of technological change.

CASE STUDY 10

*Introducing a minicomputer into the accounts department of a small company*

| | |
|---|---|
| *Company:* | Oil distribution company |
| *Department:* | Accounts |
| *Staff:* | 9 (male and female) |
| *Change:* | Introducing a minicomputer |

### Background

In this case the company was an authorised distributor for a major oil producer. It operated in several areas in Northern England. A total of 63 personnel were employed, some in the head office and others working from the four depots.

The accounts section was responsible for normal accounting functions including credit control. The accountant had responsible to him an accounting supervisor and a credit control supervisor. Four clerks worked in the accounts section, i.e. purchase ledger, two data processing and a cashier. In credit control there were two clerk/typists who were also required at times to work in the sales department. In total there were 20 head office staff, 15 of whom were clerical staff.

### Problem awareness

A minicomputer was being introduced which would be used to automate clerical procedures wherever technically possible and economically viable. The system to be installed was to be similar to one already functioning in another authorised distributor's offices.

### Diagnosis

The manager viewed many of the existing jobs as repetitive in nature with employees normally working in one job only. They found this work boring, a factor which was believed to contribute to a high error rate. Two clerk/typists were required to work mostly in credit control, but additionally at times they had to assist in the sales department. Whilst this created more variety, a factor leading to increased interest, it appeared to create anxiety about completion of tasks for which they were definitely responsible as well as uncertainty about reporting relationships. A consequence of this seemed to be 'friction' between employees.

Computerisation of the clerical function was likely to create jobs comprising work which would be more repetitive in nature. Additionally, there would be staff reductions. Anticipation of staff changes appeared to be contributing to a general lowering of morale. At the time no decisions had been made regarding reductions in staff numbers.

## Change planning

The action plan developed at the workshop contained five steps:

1    Discussions with other authorised distributors about installing computer systems, particularly technical and personnel problems encountered, and actions taken to resolve the issues. A continuing dialogue was then to be maintained with these other distributors throughout implementation.
2    Examine redeployment opportunities for staff.
3    Involve staff during the period of change in order to develop understanding, skills and competence.
4    Arrange office so as to create a friendly atmosphere and increased job interest for the period after the 'novelty' of computers has worn off.
5    Allocate new jobs in such a way as to maintain variety in the jobs.

Contact with the manager six months following the workshop revealed that no progress had been made. The minicomputer had not been installed at that stage.

---

**DISCUSSION POINTS**

1    Discussions with staff from other companies where similar change in technology has been introduced will assist in the identification of personnel problems and

---

possible means for avoiding or overcoming these problems.

2    Early anticipation of staff reductions enables managers to assist staff more effectively. Career counselling, training and redeployment can be planned and undertaken more effectively.

# CASE STUDY 11

*Organisation and methods investigation of an international sales administration department*

| | |
|---|---|
| *Company:* | Oil products marketing company |
| *Department:* | International sales administration |
| *Staff:* | 11 (male and female) including manager |
| *Change:* | O&M investigation into clerical procedures |

## Background

The department forming the basis for this case study was the international sales administration department of a company that produces, distributes and markets blended oils and greases. The participant at the workshop was a management services officer involved in an investigation within the department.

Within the department a manager was responsible for two supervisors, four clerks and four clerk/typists. The department was organised into two sections, one responsible for shipping, the other for accounts. The supervisors were both in their forties, one male and the other female. Subordinates were all less than 25 years old.

The shipping section processed orders – order received, financial checks undertaken, supply selected, invoice raised. There were 13 suppliers, six UK-based, two UK stores and five overseas blenders. Decisions about supply were complex. It is the complexity rather than the volume of work which was seen to be a source of problems. The task was made more complex because of the different international trade regulations and procedures to be complied with.

## Problem awareness and diagnosis

Clerks experienced frustration resulting from their inability to influence other departments upon whom they depended for supply and financial data. Temporary workers were often required to cover for sickness, holidays and staff shortages. Clerks were relatively inexperienced and consequently the supervisors tended to feel the need to retain detailed information about the work. The demands of the job did not permit staff the time to develop improved methods.

In the longer term, growth in sales was anticipated at 100 per cent over five years. Longer term, a need was perceived to develop the skills and abilities of younger staff to replace older employees nearing retirement.

The O&M officer had undertaken a survey of workloads associated with other departments and the problems of liaison. A reallocation of workload to the stock controller being made responsible for overseas stores. Also a liaison contract person was appointed to deal with the interface between departments.

### Change planning

The action plan proposed the following steps:

1   Gain commitment from staff on need for analysis of work-load and study of situation; use volume increase as motive and develop relationship with supervisors.
2   Document their clerical systems and isolate duplication and short cuts.
3   Sell ideas to supervisors and gain agreement on problem areas.
4   Identify problems and agree on solution:

| Improve efficiency | — computerise invoicing and statistics |
| | — merge shipping and accounts staff |
| | — minimise errors through training and continuity of experience |
| | — delegate responsibility and room for job interest to clerical-level staff |
| Reduce workload | — take some jobs in finance-and production-related areas away |

5   Establish a work group atmosphere of team and not as now with no delegation and involvement.

Soon after the workshop the O&M officer was moved to a different job. Within six months of the workshop he had moved to another organisation and follow-up was not possible.

## DISCUSSION POINTS

1   O&M studies can be 'sold' to the manager and staff or alternatively O&M can be a joint exercise involving group problem-solving.

2   Where complex decisions are required or complex systems have to be operated performance is dependent upon staff of high skill and experience. High staff turnover results in increased dependence upon the 'core' of longer-service employees. It may result in frustration but is a way also of the 'core' maintaining the organisation's dependency.

*Telephone and mail order clerks*

| | |
|---|---|
| *Company:* | Oil blending company |
| *Department:* | Order department |
| *Staff:* | Male supervisor and female clerks |
| *Change:* | Preliminary study concerned with introducing computer systems |

### Background

The order section of a company blending and marketing lubricants and other oil formed the basis for this case study. The workshop participant was the company training officer with responsibilities also for some O&M investigations.

In this section orders were received by telephone and through the mail, details were checked with the customer's card and orders raised. Female clerks in the department reported to a young male supervisor. Their work consisted of checking and updating customer cards, preparing name and address plates and addresses on order documents and actually typing the order sets.

### Problem awareness and diagnosis

The training manager had noted a general indifference amongst staff. He felt that this was resulting in poor output and a high error rate. Also staff were observed as not using initiative. The management did not believe that the supervisor was satisfactory. Equipment and systems were generally outdated and the office was overcrowded. New computer systems being introduced were causing concern amongst staff about their future role.

### Change planning

The manager established the objectives in his action plan as:

1   Update and maintain large computer record file ready for computer input.
2   Ensure new computerised system is designed in such a way that boredom and lack of interest does not produce errors, create indifference or restrict output.

Actions proposed included:

a   Commit computer department to providing facilities for interim system.
b   Restore order office confidence to availability and efficiency of computer.
c   Combine customer contact aspects with order preparation to provide a complete job.

No information was made available about progress.

---

### DISCUSSION POINTS

1   Staff are more likely to be dissatisfied in a poorly organised and run office than *vice versa*.

2   Jobs can result following computer system design, or alternatively local management can attempt to influence the systems designer to ensure that preferred principles for the design of jobs and work organisation are incorporated into the overall systems design.

---

# Bibliography

The following books will give a helpful further introduction to the following subjects.

## New technology and its implications

Cecil, P.B., *Management of Word Processing Operations,* Addison-Wesley, New York (August 1980).

Forester, T., *The Microelectronics Revolution,* Blackwell, Oxford (1980).

McCabe, H.M., and Popham, E.L., *Word Processing: A Systems Approach to the Office,* Harcourt Brace Javanovich, New York (1977).

Price, S.G., *Introducing the Electronic Office,* National Computing Centre, London (1979).

Spencer, D.D., *Computers in Action: How Computers Work,* Hayden, New Jersey (1978).

## Approaches to managing technological change

Birchall, D.W., *Job Design – A Planning and Implementation Guide for Managers,* Gower Press, Farnborough (1975).

Cakir, A., Hart, D.J., and Stewart, T.F.M., *The VDT Manual,* University of Loughborough (1978).

Davis, L.E., and Taylor, J.C., *Design of Jobs,* Penguin (1972).

Legge, K., and Mumford, E., *Designing Organisations for Satisfaction and Efficiency,* Gower Press, Farnborough (1978).

Mumford, E., and Henshal,, D., *A Participative Approach to Computer Systems Design,* Associated Business Press, London (1979).

## A trade union perspective

APEX, *Office Technology: the Trade Union Response,* Association of Professional, Executive, Clerical and Computer Staff, London (1979).

APEX, *Automation and the Office Worker,* Association of Professional, Executive, Clerical and Computer Staff, London (1980).

FEIT, *Computers and Work – FEIT Action Programme,* International Federation of Commercial, Clerical and Technical Employees, Geneva (1979).

Jenkins, C., and Sherman, B., *The Collapse of Work,* Eyre Methuen, London (1979).


## Motivation and job satisfaction

Herzberg, F., *Work and the Nature of Man,* World Publishing Co., Cleveland (1966).

Lawler, E.E., *Motivation in Work Organisations,* Brooks/Cole, Monterey California (1973).

Schein, E., *Organizational Psychology,* Prentice-Hall, New Jersey (1972).

Steers, R.M., and Porter, L.W., *Motivation and Work Behavior,* McGraw-Hill, New York (1979).

Vroom, V.H., *Work and Motivation,* John Wiley, New York (1964).

# Glossary

*Alphanumeric*   Containing both the letters of the alphabet and the numerals 0-9.

*American National Standards Institute (ANSI)*   The body that has been particularly active with regard to comuter programming languages.

*Augment*   Computer conferencing system marketed by Tymshare in USA. This system enables voice conferencing to be supplemented by text and data screened on a computer terminal as an aid to discussion.

*Automatic typewriter*   A typewriter that captures keystrokes on magnetic media, such as magnetic cards or cassettes, for automatic playback. Offers minimal editing facilities. Used for rapid production of semi-standard letters and similar work.

*Batch*   A collection of similar work which can be processed at one time (as in *batch processing* on the computer).

*British Standards Institute (BSI)*   The UK body responsible for standards in a wide range of activities including office equipment and data processing.

*Cartridge*   A plastic or metal container holding magnetic tape used with magnetic tape selectric typewriters.

*Cassette*   A container of magnetic tape used with some forms of dictation equipment and also with some types of word processor.

*Ceefax*   The teletext service offered by the British Broadcasting Corporation. It is a receive-only system. Subscribers can order a quantity of pages to appear sequentially on the television screen.

*Central processing unit (CPU)*   The 'brains' of the computer comprising the logic and the control units.

*Command*   The instruction to a machine, e.g. word processor, to carry out a particular action.

*Command key*   The key on, for example, a word processor keyboard which, when hit, intructs the program to carry out a particular action.

*Communicating printer*   A word processor or computer that can send and receive text from compatible systems over telephone lines.

*Communicating typewriter*   As Communicating printer.

*Computer*   Electronic equipment consisting of a central processing unit, input and output and storage devices, which can perform multiple complex calculation or logic operations.

*Computer output microfilm (COM)*   Computer-produced microfilm or microfiche.

*Conferencing systems*   A number of different types of system are available, e.g. voice conferencing using the telephone networks; video conferencing both with continuous transmission (for pictures and sound as in Confravision) or with snapshot transmission which is more suitable for documents; computer conferencing, both screen sharing — see *Augment* for an example, and file sharing, see *Planet/Forum* for an example.

*Confravision*   Video conferencing service with continuous television pictures and sound, offered by the British Post Office in several major cities in the UK. The service will also be provided on companies' own premises.

*Cursor*   The movable dot or other symbol on a word processor screen which shows the place on the displayed document for making a change or entering new text.

*Daisy wheel*   A high-quality print element used in word processing. It is a plastic disk in the shape of a daisy flower head with one character on each of the 96 petals. Metallised versions are available for better quality. The wheel can be interchanged to provided different type faces.

*Data processing*   Term used to describe the function of handling the mass of data involved in the transactions related to a firm's business — usually used in relation to computerised data processing. It may also be called electronic data processing. Both these terms could now be contrasted with word processing which tends to deal with text rather than transactions.

*Editing*   Revising and correcting text on a word processor, reading, scanning, deleting, inserting and reformatting text.

*Electronic data processing*   See *Data processing*.

*Electronic mail*   Communications transmitted using telecommunication systems between distant locations. The data is transmitted in digital code and recreated in readable form at the destination. Communication may be between communicating typewriters, computers, systems such as telex and facsimile, but for full electronic mail all items must be address-coded and the system must be capable of delivering to that address-code.

*Electronic typewriter*   A typewriter that operates electronically and which offers limited storage and editing facilities but sometimes has the potential of being upgraded to a full word-processing facility.

*Element*   Used in word processing to refer to the typing head component. See *Daisy wheel* for an example.

*Facsimile*   A scanning device that transmits by radio, but more commonly in offices by telephone, printed or graphic material. It transmits one page at a time for reproduction at the other end.

*Floppy disk*   A magnetic disk, looking like a gramaphone record, on which information can be stored and retrieved by random access. Depending on the size of the floppy disk, it holds between 24 and 200 pages of A4 text. The term 'floppy' is used to distinguish these disks from the 'rigid' disk which is used for computer memories and for some word processors.

*Global replace*   Term used in word processing for the facility that allows a particular item or phrase to be changed throughout a document with a single instruction.

*Hard copy*   Written, typed or printed matter — a document.

*Hardware*   The mechanical, electronic parts of central processing units in computing and word processing systems. (As opposed to *software*.)

*I/O*   Input/output.

*IT*   Information technology or informatics, a generic term used to describe equipment used to process, transmit or otherwise handle information in the widest sense, also systems and procedures related thereto.

*Information bases*   Large stores of information held on computer and accessed through terminals or visual display units. The information is usually available on a menu approach, i.e. the searcher is prompted to clarify the enquiry. This discipline allows successful searches at high speed through very large volumes of information. Examples of information bases are the British Library Automated Information Services (BLAISE) and the Chemical Society of America (Chemical Abstracts).

*International Organization for Standardization (ISO)*   The body that aims to establish international standards and to co-ordinate national ones.

*Ink jet printer*   High-quality printing technique used in word processing. The characters are formed by a controlled jet of quick-drying ink. The type face can be varied by program controls.

*Justification*   The adjustment of spacing in a line of type to produce a straight right-hand, as well as left-hand, margin. More than one kind of justification is available: refined justification which spreads the space so that there are no 'rivers' of white space in the text, is to be preferred.

*Keyboard*  An arrangement of alphanumeric keys as on a typewriter. On word processors there are additional keys, especially functional keys, which instruct the machine to perform certain tasks, e.g. print. There may also be calculating keys as on mini- and microcomputers.

*Keyboarding*  The act of using a keyboard, i.e. similar to typing but also being able to use the other functional keys.

*Keypunch*  A machine with a typewriter-like keyboard used to prepare data for the computer by punching codes in pre-assigned cards. Codes are transferred to the cards by keypunch operators.

*Language*  Computer language is the code by which the programmer communicates with the computer. Two types of language are commonly described with regard to computers:
*High level* – e.g. COBAL and BASIC, which looks very similar to English and is easy to understand but which makes more demands on the computer.
*Low level* – e.g. Assembler, which is complex to learn because it requires a detailed knowledge of computing but is more efficient in terms of the computer power used.
As the cost of computer processing falls it will become relatively less of a problem to use high-level languages and one would expect to see more of these and the gulf widening between users who can work with the machines in high-level languages and the technical programmers who use the low-level languages for master operations.

*Laser scanners*  A laser beam controlled by a microprocessor which can scan text and convert it to printed output.

*Logic unit*  That part of the central processing unit which is mainly responsible for processing programs.

*Mag*  Abbreviation for magnetic.

*Mag card/Mag tape*  Card or tape coated with magnetic material on which information can be stored. Magnetic tape is also used as recording media in dictating machines.

*Magnetic ink character readers (MICR)*  See *OCR*.

*Mainframe computers*  Large powerful computer using a sophisticated range of languages and software. It is used for very large volumes of data.

*Maltron keyboard*  Ergonomically designed keyboard for typewriter and similar machines.

*Media*  In computing and word-processing terminology this refers to the material on which information is stored, e.g. paper tape, magnetic cards, tapes, disks.

*Memory*   The store of information on a computer or word processor. The memory can be within the computer by means of a circuit, or it can be separate, e.g. on floppy or rigid disks.

*Memory typewriter*   A typewriter that stores keyboarded material (small volumes) and plays it back automatically. See also *Automatic* and *Electronic typewriters*.

*Merge*   Combining information from two memories, e.g. tapes or disks, as for producing personalised letters from standard text and address lists on a word processor.

*Microcomputer*   A very small computer based on the technology of the microprocessor.

*Microelectronics*   General term for manufacture and use of highly sophisticated miniaturised electronic circuits.

*Microfiche*   A sheet of rigid plastic on which is reproduced many pages of information. It must be read through a viewer but usually each sheet has printed on it identification data which can be read without magnification.

*Microfilm*   Film on which is stored information greatly reduced from the original. Again, a viewer is needed. The film is stored as a roll and may be in a cassette.

*Micrographics*   The science, art and technology by which information is quickly reduced in size on microfilm or microfiche for easy storage and retrieval.

*Microprocessor*   The central processing unit of a microcomputer — a silicon chip. Widely used in office technology as the 'drive' mechanism.

*Minicomputer*   A medium-power computer with a narrow range of languages but considerable storage and processing capacity.

*Modem*   Abbreviation for 'modulator-demodulator'. This is a device that varies the characteristics of signals transmitted via communications facilities.

*OCR: Optical character recognition (or reader)*   A scanning device and magnetic ink character reader that converts already printed or written material into a form suitable for storing on the computer or word processor for later retrieval.

*Office technology*   The general term used to describe the machines and equipment used to carry out office work and procedures.

*Off-line*   A peripheral device operated independent of the central processor.

*On-line*   Connected directly to the main processor either through or by a cable.

*Oracle*   The teletext service offered by the International Broadcasting Authority in UK. Similar to Ceefax, it is a receive-only system. Subscribers can order a quantity of pages to appear on the television screen.

*PABX (Private automatic branch exchange)*   Machinery which switches calls between the public telephone network and internal extensions. Can also be used for a central dictating service.

*PBX (Private branch exchange)*   Telephone switchboard with a human operator.

*Pagination*   A feature on some word processors which allows pages to be numbered and ejected automatically during playout.

*Paper tape*   Used to record information on some word processors and computing systems. The punched perforations in the tape carry the coding.

*Peripherals*   Equipment in data processing or word processing that works in conjunction with the central processing unit but is not an integral part. Examples include terminal keyboards, printers, OCR.

*Photocomposition*   A text production process in which characters are exposed photographically on light-sensitive paper which is then developed to become a reproduction-quality proof.

*Planet/Forum*   Computer conferencing system available on the value-added network in USA. This system allows participants to share a discussion and to continue to access and add to the debate over weeks or months by updating personal and conference files.

*Prestel*   Computer-based information system operated by the Post Office in UK. Access is via telephone link and output is on a television receiver. It can be interrogated directly by the viewer and is an example of a viewdata service.

*Printer*   The unit which types out a page, e.g. a typewriter or a line printer.

*Printwheel*   A typing element used on some word processors. A daisy wheel is an example.

*Program*   Set of machine instructions for the operation of automated equipment such as computers and word processors.

*Programmer*   One who creates programs — usually computer programmer.

*Proofreading*   Reading copy to detect and mark errors which are to be corrected.

*Proportional spacing*   A feature on some typewriters which gives the characters horizontal space in line with proportions one with another, i.e. the letter 'i' is given less space than the letter 'm'.

*Qwerty keyboard*   The usual layout for a typewriter-type keyboard. It is named after the layout of letters, top left alpha. Although this keyboard was not laid out for fast typing is has become so accepted, it is difficult to bring about changes to faster keyboards such as the *Maltron* which is ergonomically designed.

*RAM*   Random access memory.

*ROM*   Read-only memory.

*Random access*   A storage technique in word processing and data processing which allows access to individual items randomly in a fraction of a second as compared with the serial nature of tape storage.

*Read-only memory*   A memory onto which information is written and which cannot then be altered.

*Reprographics*   Reproduction and duplication of documents by photocopy, offset printing, microfilming, office duplicating.

*Screen*   Cathode ray tube used to display information on word processors, for example.

*Shared logic*   Term used for a text-editing system where several keyboards and terminals simultaneously use the memory and processing power of one central processor.

*Silicon chip*   Printed circuits, reduced photoelectronically and printed on a thin wafer of silicon. The wafers are built up until thousands of circuits are maintained in a small chip of silicon. This then is used as a microprocessor.

*Software*   Materials needed to control and operate the hardware of a computer or word processor, e.g. flowcharts, manuals, *programs.*

*Stand-alone*   Description of word processor which is complete in itself, not connected to other units.

*Storage media*   See *Media.*

*Technology*   The way or means of accomplishing a task. The technology may or may not include the use of machines. In office technology the term implies the use of equipment to carry out office systems and procedures.

*Telecommunications*   The science that deals with the study of communication at a distance, as by radio, telegraphy, telephone, television.

*Teleprinter/telex*   A machine with a keyboard which is operated by a teletypist who telephones another similar operator in a distant location. Once the connection is made, the two teletypists can communicate by typing while the machine records their message in writing.

*Teleprocessing*   The form of communication processing in which a word or data processing system utilises communication facilities.

*Teletex*   The proposed international telecommunications service which would be administered by the telephone networks. It would offer fast, reliable links with word processors and other office activities. It could replace telex in the longer term.

*Teletext*  Broadcast information systems in UK. Ceefax and Oracle are examples.

*Telex*  See *Teleprinter*

*Terminals*  A work station which can interface directly with the computer. It usually has a keyboard and may have a screen.

*Text*  Used in this context as the output of a word processing system.

*Value added network (VAN) services*  Communications services which do more than transmit information. These systems manipulate, translate, re-order or store information on behalf of the sender or the recipient. They can be used to provide computer conferencing facilities. At present they are used extensively in the USA and to some extent in Europe via the public postal and telephone authorities.

*Viewdata*  Generic name for systems allowing access to large volumes of computer stored information via telecommunications networks. Prestel is an example.

*Visual display unit, visual display terminal (VDU, VDT)*  Devices similar to a television screen which are used to display information or data electronically. They are attached to computer or word-processing systems.

*Word processing*  The combination of people, procedures and equipment that transforms ideas into printed communications to help facilitate the flow of related office work. It offers a means of producing written communication at high speed, with greater accuracy and at lower cost.

*Word processors*  The electronic equipment used to prepare, store and retrieve text. Word processors range from simple editing typewriters to advanced systems linked to a central computer and to others which can communicate with each other.

# Index

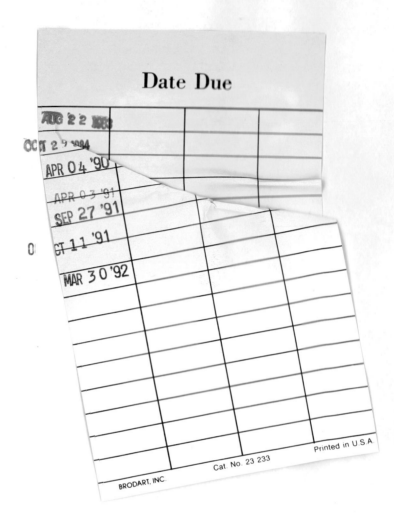

# Date Due

| | | |
|---|---|---|
| AUG 22 1988 | | |
| OCT 2 9 1994 | | |
| APR 04 '90 | | |
| APR 03 '91 | | |
| SEP 27 '91 | | |
| OCT 11 '91 | | |
| MAR 30 '92 | | |
| | | |
| | | |
| | | |
| | | |
| | | |
| | | |
| | | |
| | | |

BRODART, INC.  Cat. No. 23 233  Printed in U.S.A.